To David

Very Best Wishes

Alan Fine

You Already
Know How to Be Great

You **ALREADY** Know How to Be **GREAT**

A Simple Way to Remove Interference and Unlock Your Greatest Potential

ALAN FINE

with **REBECCA R. MERRILL**

PORTFOLIO / PENGUIN

PORTFOLIO PENGUIN

Published by the Penguin Group

Penguin Group (USA) Inc., 375 Hudson Street, New York, New York 10014, U.S.A.

Penguin Group (Canada), 90 Eglinton Avenue East, Suite 700,

Toronto, Ontario, Canada M4P 2Y3 (a division of Pearson Penguin Canada Inc.)

Penguin Books Ltd, 80 Strand, London WC2R 0RL, England

Penguin Ireland, 25 St. Stephen's Green, Dublin 2, Ireland (a division of Penguin Books Ltd)

Penguin Books Australia Ltd, 250 Camberwell Road, Camberwell, Victoria 3124, Australia

(a division of Pearson Australia Group Pty Ltd)

Penguin Books India Pvt Ltd, 11 Community Centre, Panchsheel Park,

New Delhi – 110 017, India

Penguin Group (NZ), 67 Apollo Drive, Rosedale, North Shore 0632, New Zealand

(a division of Pearson New Zealand Ltd)

Penguin Books (South Africa) (Pty) Ltd, 24 Sturdee Avenue, Rosebank, Johannesburg 2196,

South Africa

Penguin Books Ltd, Registered Offices:

80 Strand, London WC2R 0RL, England

First published in 2010 by Portfolio Penguin,

a member of Penguin Group (USA) Inc.

10   9

Illustration on page 3 used by permission of Root Learning

CIP data available

ISBN 978-1-59184-355-9

Printed in the United States of America

Set in New Caledonia, with display in Century Schoolbook, Clarendon, and Helvetica Neue

Designed by BTDNYC

To all those amazing people

*who make it safe for others to explore
their own experience—especially those
who did and still do it for me*

CONTENTS

Part 1
PARADIGM AND PRINCIPLE

CHAPTER ONE

*Why gaining more knowledge is not necessarily the key to being a
better manager, leader, employee, parent, or individual performer*

CHAPTER TWO

*The three innate elements of top performance that facilitate the use of
knowledge (Faith, Fire, and Focus) and how you can unleash them*

CHAPTER THREE

*What's getting in the way of breakthrough performance
and how to remove it*

Part 2

PROCESS

Part 3

PRACTICE

FOREWORD

by Stephen R. Covey

Over the years, one of the most important ideas I've learned about and taught is the power of a "paradigm shift"—of seeing something in a new and different way that creates a huge change in thinking and behavior.

In *You Already Know How to Be Great,* Alan Fine creates a paradigm shift of major proportion. Most often, he says, dramatic performance improvement does not come from gaining new knowledge; it comes from getting rid of the "interference" that gets in the way of using the knowledge and capacity we already have. That one idea has phenomenal implications and applications. It literally transforms the way we approach improving our own performance and also the way we approach helping others improve theirs.

Five Reasons Why I Like This Book

There are a number of reasons why Alan's approach resonates with my passion for effectiveness in leadership and in life.

TO BEGIN WITH, it taps into two fundamental human desires that are deep within each of us—the desire to be and do our best and the desire to be significant to others, to make a difference. These desires created a catalyst for my own work on *The 8th Habit*—"Find Your Voice and Inspire Others to Find Theirs." In *You Already Know,* Alan shares a paradigm and a process to help readers fulfill these basic desires by improving their own performance in any area of life and also helping others to improve theirs.

SECOND, it's not some fad or "flavor of the month." It's based on sound, universal principles. For example, Alan's approach recognizes top performance only comes when the *performer,* not the coach (or leader or manager or teacher or parent), proactively accepts responsibility for results. This frees individuals to release their talent and creativity and increase their performance capacity.

THIRD, this approach is highly pragmatic. It not only acknowledges the principles of breakthrough performance; it provides both the performer and the "coach" a simple but robust way to implement them through Alan's GROW process.

FOURTH, it stands solidly apart from approaches that while they enable people to perform in the moment create a dependency on the advice and direction of others. Truly great leaders, great managers, great coaches, and great parents help others strengthen their core capacity, thus empowering them to be effective not only in the moment but also in multiple applications over time.

FIFTH, this approach is universally applicable. It provides a template that can help *any* individual improve performance in *any* area of life. It can help *any* group or team resolve *any* issue and improve performance in *any* organization. One of the important implications is that this truly is an approach for a global world.

I'm excited by the insight this book provides into the nature of human performance and how to influence it in self and in others. I'm even more excited by the language Alan has developed to help people understand and talk about performance issues and by the simple, highly pragmatic tools he has created to address them. But most of all, I'm excited by the results. There are a lot of people with a lot of good ideas for making the world better. But Alan is one who's been able to translate ideas into simple doable actions that truly create breakthrough outcomes.

To me, this book is really a book about leadership—both personal and public. It gives readers the vision and the tools to exercise personal leadership by improving their own performance and public leadership by helping others improve theirs. In doing so, it helps readers walk an enriching path of fulfillment and contribution. It is a truly landmark book on helping yourself and others journey to greatness.

UP FRONT

If we did the things we are capable of doing, we would literally astound ourselves.

THOMAS A. EDISON,
American inventor and businessman

Do any of these scenarios sound familiar?

- You know that if you had a regular exercise program you'd have more energy and feel better. You've bought a variety of exercise equipment. You've tried a lot of different types of programs. Each time, you've lasted about three weeks. You ask yourself: "What's the matter with me? Do I just not have the character to do this—or was I somewhere else when the exercise genes got passed out?"

- You've been told that your job as a manager includes coaching the people in your division, so you've been meeting with them regularly, giving them good instruction and trying to help them improve. But much of the time, your help doesn't seem to matter, and sometimes it's even rejected. One person you need to talk with about an accountability issue refuses to even meet with you. You think: "How can I coach these people, and how can I do it in a way that will truly make a difference?"

- You're trying to help your daughter grow up to be a responsible adult, but you can't even get her to clean her room. You've tried everything— incentives, encouragement, punishment, withdrawal of privileges, even yelling—but nothing seems to work. You wonder: "What's it going to take to make her want to keep her room clean?"

- You're standing on the golf course at the first tee. You're playing with some clients, and you'd really like to make a good impression. You know what it's like to hit a really nice drive, but you can't do it consistently. So you worry: "What if I hit the ball into the trees or 'whiff' it? What are these people going to think?"

- Your organization is not performing as well as you'd like. You've tried a variety of approaches and had some success, but the goals you set at the top never really make it down the line and your employees are not fully engaged. You spend most of your days dealing with internal problems instead of external opportunities. You keep asking yourself: "How can I raise performance throughout the organization? What can I do to get everyone fully engaged and on the same page?"

These scenarios represent a wide range of common experience, but they have one important element in common: they all deal with issues of performance—either in self or in others. Most of us want the results of top performance. We want the enthused organization, the engaged work team, the exceeded sales quotas, the responsible child, the low handicap on the golf course, the increased energy and the washboard abs. But even when we know what it takes, we don't always have the tools that make those kinds of results possible.

This book is about those tools. It's about a paradigm, a principle, and a process that can lead to breakthrough performance in the workplace, on the golf course, in the boardroom, in the family room, or anyplace where higher performance makes a difference. It's about how to improve performance in your own life and also in the lives of those you are trying to help. It's based on the premise that

> EVERYONE has the potential to perform better;
> potential is blocked by interference;
> interference can be reduced by focused attention; and
> focused attention can be simply and systematically increased.

Let Me Introduce Myself

My name is Alan Fine. I began my career teaching tennis in Wales. In my search to be a better coach, I stumbled onto a paradigm of human performance and a simple process to improve it that have led me to successfully coach CEOs, managers, and leaders in organizations worldwide, as well as world-class golfers such as David Feherty, Colin Montgomerie, Phil Price, and Stephen Ames.

The primary focus of my company—InsideOut Development—is working with business leaders and managers, and that's what I've spent most of the past twenty-five years doing. But I've also been thrilled to see how people immediately apply these principles in other areas, including parenting, sports, hobbies, and the performing arts. As many have observed, this "whole life" approach consistently reinforces the paradigm and process, making it significantly easier to improve performance both on and off the job.

As I've worked with these ideas over the years, two things have become clear to me:

1. When we don't understand the nature of human performance, we tend to diagnose performance problems and come up with solutions from a perspective that represents only a fraction of what it takes to be a top performer; and the solutions we come up with typically do not sustain long-term performance improvement.

2. If we don't have a way to consistently make quick, accurate decisions and execute them well in today's fast-paced global economy, we're going to be left in the dust.

This book can help you both understand human performance and make quick, accurate decisions in moving ahead. It will give you a simple, effective paradigm and a scalable, replicable process that will enable you to consistently improve performance in any area of life.

My Invitation to You

You Already Know How to Be Great has been written in response to the many requests I have received over the years to put the inside-out performance principles into writing. It reflects my ongoing quest to make these principles highly practical and simple to apply in everyday life.

My invitation to you is to simply play with the ideas in these pages and use what's helpful to you. As you will discover, this book is less about gaining new knowledge and more about getting rid of what's keeping you from using the knowledge you already have. It's less about doing new things and more about understanding and giving language and order to some of the great things you already do, so that you can do those things more consistently and with better results.

I encourage you to approach this book in whatever way you feel will work best for you. If you like supportive research and quotes, check out the call-out boxes. If you want to give the content deeper personal thought, go through the

Reflective Questions at the end of each chapter. If you prefer to skip the research and questions, just read the text. I do recommend that you pay particular attention to each of the stories. They represent the "live" research for this book. They come from people who have had experience with this material not only in their organizations but also in their personal lives. Because the fundamental ideas are based on principles, even if you don't happen to be a manager or a leader or a teacher or a parent now, you'll find the insights shared by these individuals can be applied in almost any situation. Besides, you never know when you might end up in one of these roles.

I also invite you to check out the You Already Know How to Be Great online community at www.alan-fine.com, where you can find additional examples, exercises, and tools to help you apply the principles in each chapter of this book. Within the community, you'll also be able to learn from the experiences of others and share your own experiences so that others can learn from you. I've placed a link at the end of each chapter as a reminder of this additional resource.

I'm excited to share these principles and tools with you. I certainly don't have all the answers. And I'm not suggesting that what's in this book is a panacea for every performance issue. But in years of coaching, I've become convinced that understanding some essential elements of human performance and having a simple process to influence those elements can help you achieve your greatness in any arena. My guess is that deep inside, you—and the people you're trying to help—have nurtured some dreams of what's possible in life, but that "stuff" has gotten in the way of realizing those dreams. It's my hope that this book will help you get rid of the "stuff" and free you—and those you help—to make those dreams come true.

ALAN FINE

Part 1

PARADIGM
and
PRINCIPLE

A Blinding Glimpse of the **OBVIOUS**

As I look back, it seems that everything was gray—the sky, the pavement, the walls surrounding the pavement, the castlelike building with its turret-topped roof, even the endless terraced rows of tiny, two-up, two-down houses outside the walls. From a distance, there was no indication that this very gray place—the Mackintosh Tennis Club—was the home of some of the best tennis players in Wales. There was also no indication that this place would become the scene of one of the greatest epiphanies of my life or that it would open the door for me to help managers, leaders, salespeople, athletes, teachers, musicians, parents, and others around the world achieve breakthrough performance.

The journey that led me to this place on that eventful morning was something of a fluke. It had begun years before when I was eleven and my brother entered me as a contestant in our school tennis tournament. I was a severely asthmatic, skinny, and painfully shy kid, and up to that point, I'd only been on a tennis court three times in my life. Somehow I found myself in the finals and discovered I was up against a thirteen-year-old who was six feet tall and captain of the rugby team—the school "jock." To this day, I can remember exactly where I was standing on the court when I suddenly realized that I was ahead, 6–4, 4–0. I remember a voice in my head saying, "Okay, you've won ten games.

You only have to win two more, and you'll be the school champion! How hard can that be?" Suddenly I froze. I didn't win another game. The jock beat me 6–0 in the final set. I could feel the disappointment of my PE instructor all the way from across the court and up on the second tier of the playground. I could sense the kids who had been watching whispering, "Wow! What happened to him?" All I could think in that moment was, "Please, please don't let me cry!"

Though I was mortified by the defeat, from that day I decided to take up tennis with a vengeance. For the first time in my life, I'd found something that both my peers and the adults in my life recognized me for.

During the next few years, one of the local sports administrators took me under his wing. He took me to training programs for tennis coaches where I got to be the guinea pig for the trainee coaches. It was there that I learned a lot about what did and didn't work in coaching. After graduation from high school, I went on to college and studied optometry for two years. At the same time, I began using what I'd learned from the trainees to teach tennis on the side. Unfortunately (or maybe fortunately), I was thrown out of college for spending too much time teaching tennis. So I decided to do the training necessary to qualify as a Registered Professional Coach, which was the highest tennis-teaching certification a person could get in the UK at the time.

It was as a certified coach eight years later that I stood on the court on that gray day that totally changed my life. I had been working with one of my students—a shy little nine-year-old girl. Her mother and I both agreed that she was a bit uncoordinated, but her mom felt that if I could help her improve a little, she would be able to participate in the group sessions, which would be very good for her socially. The instructions I'd given her had been very simple ("Shake hands with your racket." "Hit the ball on its way down." "Hit the back side of the ball."). But the best she'd been able to do was to hit the ball about five times consecutively across the net.

Feeling frustrated as I watched her struggle, I decided to try something different. I'd just begun to expand my approach to coaching, including studying disciplines such as Neuro-Linguistic Programming™ (NLP™), psychosynthesis, Zen, and everything I could find on sports psychology. One particular approach that caught my attention was Timothy Gallwey's *Inner Game of Tennis*. The basic idea is that we each have a Self 1, the analytical, critical self ("You didn't hold the racket right." "You should have hit that differently." "You moved too slowly, you dummy!"), and a Self 2, the natural, curious self that learns by experience and performs best without the interference of Self 1.

Performance improves when we're basically able to silence Self 1 and free Self 2 to do its thing.

So I said to this little girl, "Look, let's not worry about all the instructions I've given you over the past six weeks. Just say 'bounce' when the ball touches the ground and 'hit' when the ball hits your racket. That's all. Just focus on those two events. Don't worry about anything else." The first time she tried it, she hit fifty-three shots in a row over the net! The girl was thrilled. Her mother was so shocked she literally fell off her chair leaning forward to watch. Personally, I was astonished and frustrated. My fundamental view as an educator had been challenged. Was it possible that much of the specific technical instruction I'd been giving my students was not only *not* helping them but was actually getting in the way?

It was at that point that I was struck with a "blinding glimpse of the obvious." This girl hadn't been performing poorly because she didn't *know* what to do; it was simply that there was too much *interference* getting in the way of her doing it! And sadly, the principal source of that interference was me.

That day on the tennis court, that little girl improved her performance by over 1000 percent, or 10X. For that reason, I've come to think of her as "the 10X girl." Can you imagine what would happen if you were to get that kind of breakthrough performance—or even a tenth of it—in your team or organization or in other areas of your life?

Outside-In

What I learned on the court that day—and have since developed and taught for more than twenty-five years—is that there is a simple paradigm (inside-out), principle (focus), and process (GROW) that can create significant—often dramatic—performance improvement in any arena of life. Prior to that day, I had believed—as most people do—that the best way to improve performance is to increase knowledge. If you want to get better, read a book. Take a class. Hire an expert. There's some bit of knowledge "out there" you don't have, and if you can just figure out how to get it, your performance will dramatically improve. A "formula" that reflects this approach is

$$\text{Performance} = \text{Capacity} + \text{Knowledge}$$
$$\text{or}$$
$$P = C + K$$

This is an "outside-in" (telling, didactic, instructional, directive) approach. It assumes that people are lacking in some way and that additional knowledge has to be put in from the outside to help them improve. Clearly, this is the most common approach used to improve individual and organizational performance. It reflects the fact that individuals, managers, and leaders tend to *see* performance problems as knowledge problems and therefore look for knowledge solutions.

Of course, there are times when a lack of knowledge really is the problem and circumstances in which the P = C + K formula works. *But much of the time it doesn't.* If knowledge really were all it took to be a high performer, then all any of us would have to do would be to read that book or take that class and we'd be winning golf and tennis championships. We'd all be incredible managers, great teachers, phenomenal parents and performers. But obviously we're not. Why? Because typically, **the biggest obstacle in performance isn't not knowing what to do; it's not doing what we know.** In other words, the problem is not as much about knowledge *acquisition* as it is about knowledge *execution*.

THE KNOWING-DOING GAP

In their book *The Knowing-Doing Gap*, Stanford University professors Jeffrey Pfeffer and Robert Sutton point out that thousands of books are published each year that essentially contain the same analyses and prescriptions contained in books published a year or even a decade ago. "Yet," they say, "these books have a ready market because the ideas, although often widely known and proven to be useful and valid, remain unimplemented."[1] They also point out that of the billions of dollars spent on training and consulting, most of it is on information that is being repeated—and still not implemented.

Their conclusion? "Anyone can read a book or attend a seminar. The trick is in turning the knowledge acquired into . . . action."[2]

Most of us can easily validate this in our own lives. For example, when we perform well—ace a presentation or a sales pitch, shoot a great round of golf, or play a favorite song on the piano flawlessly—we often say it's exhilarating, it's fun, it feels natural, it flows. We don't even have to think about it; it feels almost effortless. Our mind is quiet; our muscles are relaxed. But when we're performing badly, what's happening? Our muscles are tense. We have an internal dialogue going on: "Wow, that was awful! What did I do wrong? What's my problem?" So we try to analyze what we're doing wrong, and then we try hard to fix it based on our analysis. As a result, muscle tension increases. Internal dialogue increases. And typically, our performance gets even worse! So in other words, we *know* that when we're performing well, we're not using a lot of effort and not thinking about what we're doing. Yet when we're performing badly, we try to improve our performance by thinking *more* about what we're doing and using *more* effort. In other words, we do the exact opposite of what we know we do when we perform well. Why is that so?

Let's look at another example. How much of a game such as golf do you think is mental versus how much is physical or technical? When I ask this question of both professional golfers and weekend enthusiasts, the typical response is that golf is at least eighty percent mental and less than twenty percent physical or technical. Yet when I ask people how much of their practice time they actually spend rehearsing and developing their mental skills, I have yet to have anyone tell me more than 5 percent. So basically, people are saying they spend less than 5 percent of their effort on something they believe contributes 80 percent toward their performance. Something here doesn't add up!

Here's a third example. If we're in a managerial role in an organization, we may know we need to hold a performance evaluation with a poor performer. We know that if she doesn't become aware of her blind spots, she'll never improve, and we know that has consequences for her and her future as well as for the team and organization. Yet, we keep putting it off. We don't do what we know is a vital part of our job and is in the best interest of all concerned. Why?

Most of us *already know* of one thing we could do more or less of that would significantly improve our performance at work. We *already know* of something we should do to improve our personal lives, such as exercise or budget or eat better. We *already know* that if we give in to our kids' nagging for that new video game system today, we're going to regret it when they nag us even more for the latest games to go with it tomorrow. Yet, we *don't* do what we need to do to improve our performance at work; we *don't* exercise, budget, or eat better; and we *do* give

> **The problem in my life and other people's lives is not the absence of knowing what to do, but the absence of doing it.**
>
> PETER DRUCKER,
> writer, management
> consultant, social
> ecologist

in to our kids' nagging and buy that Nintendo game anyway.

Why do we behave so illogically? Knowledge alone is not what creates high performance. It's an important component, but it's not the only component. Most of the time, acquiring more knowledge will not make a difference. Closing the gap between what we know and what we do will have far greater impact on improving our performance than any additional knowledge we might gain.

Inside-Out

A different way to look at performance improvement—the way that was dramatically demonstrated to me that day with the 10X girl—is "inside-out." This approach is less about adding new knowledge and more about eliminating the interference that's getting in the way of experimenting with and using the knowledge we already have. The formula for this approach[3] is

> Execution is the great unaddressed issue in the business world today. Its absence is the single biggest obstacle to success and the cause of most of the disappointments that are mistakenly attributed to other causes.
>
> RAM CHARAN,
> business adviser,
> author, and speaker

$$Performance = Capacity - Interference$$
$$or$$
$$P = C - I$$

As I've admitted, that day on the court the primary interference to that little girl's performance was my own well-intended effort to increase her knowledge. My verbal instructions—"Shake hands with your racket," "Hit the ball on its way down," "Hit the back side of the ball"—were actually taking her focus away from what she was experiencing. She was so busy trying to listen to all the things she was being told to do "right" that she couldn't pay attention to what was actually happening.

> Experience is the most efficient teacher of all things.
>
> PLINY THE ELDER,
> 1st-century BC
> Roman scholar,
> naturalist, and
> military commander

We see the same phenomenon in organizations when managers or leaders become so obsessed with policies, procedures, and their own ways of doing things that they become disconnected from results. They begin to micromanage. They divert employees' attention away from learning and creating and toward trying to remember and comply. What an enormous loss of possibility!

Once the interference was removed from the 10X girl's awareness, she was free to focus on a critical variable* of what was happening—the location of the ball—and to learn directly from her own experience. *Most performance improvement is a direct result of this kind of learning*—processing real-time experience, unencumbered by interference. And this is just as true in the organization, the classroom, or the family as it is on the tennis court.

Even in the absence of a coach giving constant verbal instructions, interference can be created by a performer's effort to recall past instructions while trying to practice or perform. It's like trying to be in both "send" and "receive" modes on a walkie-talkie at the same time. It simply doesn't work.

TRY THIS EXPERIMENT

Hold up your hand in front of someone, and ask that person to focus on your palm. Then ask the person to think about someone he/she was with yesterday and tell you what that individual was wearing (color, style, etc.). Likely the person's eyes will glaze over or will quickly move up and to the left as he/she tries to remember. Trying to recall information stops people from focusing on the present, the here and now.

The same thing happens on the tennis court (or in any other sports venue) when a player tries to remember all the instructions he/she has been given. If a tennis ball is coming at the player at 100 miles an hour, trying to recall past instruction makes it hard to focus on what is actually happening and is a sure formula for disaster. You simply can't focus on the past and the present in the same moment.

Another way to think about it is to imagine that you're driving your car down the road with one foot on the gas pedal and the other foot on the brake. If you want to go faster, you can certainly push harder on the gas (which is the *outside-in* or "+K" approach). But as long as that other foot is on the brake,

---

*A "critical variable" is something that is constantly changing and something about which up-to-date information is vital.

you're going to get very little increase in performance and you'll burn the car out fast. On the other hand, if you simply take your foot off the brake (which

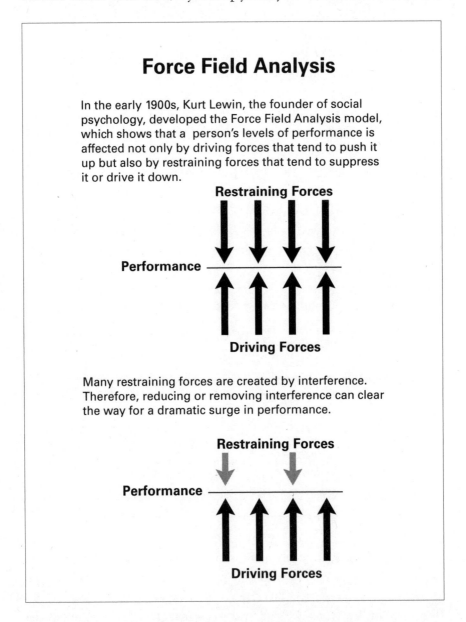

Force Field Analysis

In the early 1900s, Kurt Lewin, the founder of social psychology, developed the Force Field Analysis model, which shows that a person's levels of performance is affected not only by driving forces that tend to push it up but also by restraining forces that tend to suppress it or drive it down.

Restraining Forces

Performance

Driving Forces

Many restraining forces are created by interference. Therefore, reducing or removing interference can clear the way for a dramatic surge in performance.

Restraining Forces

Performance

Driving Forces

is the *inside-out* or "–I" approach), you can immediately get a massive increase in performance without even having to add additional knowledge or gas.

Clearly, performance improvement is not just a matter of adding knowledge. Most often, it's an issue of reducing the interference that's getting in the way of using the knowledge we already have.

A 180-Degree Turn

My experience with the 10X girl that day on the court led me to a 180-degree turn in the way I worked with my tennis students—and eventually the way I've worked with people in all kinds of organizations and many different walks of life. For one thing, it helped me realize that we're consistently forming beliefs about ourselves and other people that limit performance—people who have the same kind of potential demonstrated by that shy little girl. For example:

At work when we see . . .
- The employee who avoids accountability or doesn't seem engaged
    (We say he doesn't want to be responsible. He doesn't care about his work.)
- The boss who always has to have her way
    (We say she's arrogant. She doesn't care about what the rest of us think.)
- The colleague who resists change
    (We say he's stuck in his ways. He's probably afraid of change.)

At home when we see . . .
- The teenager who won't fulfill her responsibilities around the house
    (We say she's lazy. She doesn't care about the family.)
- The child who doesn't do his homework
    (We say he doesn't think doing well in school is important.)
- The spouse who doesn't communicate on spending
    (We say what she wants is more important to her than I am.)

In the classroom when we see . . .
- The student who sees no relevance in what the teacher is trying to teach
    (We say he's not very bright. He just doesn't "get" it.)
- The teacher who struggles to deal with a student's learning style
    (We say she's stupid and lazy; she just wants to do what's comfortable for her.)
- The student who struggles with peer relationships
    (We say he's a "loner.")

In the performing arts and sports when we see . . .

- The golfer who keeps saying, "I'm a slicer!"

    (We say she's got a negative attitude. She'll always trail the pack.)

- The musician who plays the "notes" but not the "music"

    (We say he may have some technical knowledge, but he doesn't have much talent.)

- The marathon runner whose legs turn to rubber after twenty miles

    (We say she just doesn't have what it takes to "pay the price.")

In critical performance moments when we see . . .

- The executive whose speech reads well on paper but comes over flat in front of an audience

    (We say he has no charisma. He'll never make it to the top in this organization.)

- The musician who plays well in practice and freezes up onstage

    (We say she has too much "stage fright" to ever become a top performer.)

- The student who does all the class work well but fails the exams

    (We say he'll never be a top student. When things are really on the line, he can't perform.)

We form these beliefs about others. We form them about ourselves. And these beliefs not only limit performance; they also limit the way we try to help ourselves or others improve.

The Three Performance Gaps

My experience with the 10X girl also forced me to take a deeper look at the three critical performance challenges, or "gaps," I had constantly been struggling with in trying to help people as a coach. First was the *awareness* gap. While some of my students had been swinging the racket exactly the way I told them to, others seemed to be unable to follow my instructions and would persistently swing the racket differently than I had taught. In other words, *there was a gap between what they thought they were doing and what they were actually doing.* I had thought, "These people must have some kind of learning disability. I taught them the 'correct' way to swing the racket and they're not doing it. Clearly this must be their problem—not mine!"

Second was the *pressure* gap. Watching my students who were on the national training team practice, it was difficult to tell them apart from professional players. But these students never made it past the semifinal rounds in tournaments. When the pressure was on, they choked and couldn't do what I had seen them do in practice. And I didn't seem to be able to help. Clearly, *here was another gap—a gap between how people performed in practice and how they performed under pressure.*

Third was the *expertise* gap. Like every other serious coach, I dreamed of being able to train some of the best players in the world. I believed that in order to coach someone you had to be more expert than that person—otherwise what advice could you give him/her? But since at my best, I could only play at county level (which is the equivalent of a state-ranked player in the United States), that meant I would never be able to coach anyone who played better than county level.

These same gaps show up in almost every area of our lives, including organizations. People communicate differently than they think they do. They perform well in practice but poorly under pressure. They're often called upon to supervise others who are far more expert than they are. As a result, performance rarely even approaches what's possible.

The traditional approach I'd been using of adding knowledge had done little to close these three gaps. But as I began to experiment more with removing interference, I started to notice a dramatic change in my students. Suddenly I was beginning to see them swing their rackets correctly. I saw those on the national training team start winning tournaments. And through a series of recommendations, I found myself working with professionals—including two of Britain's Davis Cup* players, who were far better players than I was—and actually helping them!

The gaps began disappearing, and I was ecstatic. But this whole experience was really shaking my fundamental beliefs about coaching. As much as it massaged my ego to think that I was the one with all this wonderful knowledge and that I could help people improve their performance by dispensing that knowledge, I was quickly beginning to realize that providing too much knowledge was actually getting in the way. I discovered that by and large, the most effective thing I could do to help others was to remove the interference that blocked their ability to learn and execute.

---

*The Davis Cup is the worldwide tennis tournament between national teams.

From Tennis Courts to Companies Worldwide

When one of the Davis Cup players I coached, Buster Mottram, moved from ninetieth to nineteenth in the world in six months, I began to receive inquiries from up-and-coming professionals on the European golf tour. They thought what I was doing might help them with their game. My first response was, "No, thanks!" I'd never played golf. (In fact, I wasn't even sure it was a proper sport, with players wearing long pants in 100-degree weather and not running around at all like they do on the tennis court!) Nevertheless, I did become involved—in good part because I enjoyed the insanity of an Irish golfer named David Feherty (whose roles as CBS broadcaster and author have since put his wit on public display) and the effervescence of David Llewellyn (the former Welsh national coach, who still holds the record for the lowest four rounds of golf ever scored in a PGA European tour event).

So then I found myself working in a field I truly knew nothing about. But through the application of the principles I was using, significant performance breakthroughs kept happening for my students. And as a result of the accompanying publicity I was asked to work in a number of other sports, including fencing, pistol shooting, swimming, running, and squash. I was also asked to work with teachers, musicians, and even with kids who were having a struggle fitting into the mainstream education system. The inside-out approach continued to create breakthrough results in every application. As I began to help executives with their sporting hobbies, some suggested that this approach might apply in their businesses as well. Subsequently, I became involved in working with executives and managers to help them improve performance in the workplace. I created a company. We made the process scalable and replicable. We began to work with organizations worldwide.

Through it all, the more I continued to read and talk with psychologists and other performance improvement experts and the more experience I had in working with people in all walks of life, the more I kept coming back to the same conclusion: *The biggest obstacle (and opportunity) in performance isn't about knowing what to do; it's about doing what we know. And what keeps us from doing what we know is interference.*

Reflective Questions

- To what extent do you typically turn to outside sources to improve your performance (new books, different approaches, another coach, the latest equipment, etc.)? What has been the result? How much has your performance actually changed?

- What are one or two things you already know you could do to significantly improve your personal or professional life that you're not doing now? What's getting in the way of your doing them?

- Think of a time when you performed well and a time when you performed badly. Compare the two experiences. What interference got in the way when you performed badly? In what specific ways did it affect your ability to perform?

- How much "interference" is getting in the way of performance in your organization, family, or team? If you're a leader, manager, or parent, is there a chance you may be creating interference and actually getting in the way of performance—no matter how well intended your efforts?

- Think about times when "pressure" causes you to perform poorly. What is it about pressure that inhibits your performance? What actually happens?

- When—and in what ways—has instruction/advice from others either inhibited or enhanced your own experience and learning?

Chapter 1: For an exercise that will help you

AIM FOR BREAKTHROUGH PERFORMANCE

Access the online community at
Alan-Fine.com

CHAPTER TWO

The Nature of Performance

Cherish that which is within you.

CHUANG-TZU,
Chinese philosopher, 4th century BCE

s I continued to work to help people and organizations improve performance, I had another blinding glimpse of the obvious. Knowledge was not the only thing—or even the most important thing—being blocked by interference. There were three other elements at the very heart of high performance. And not only were these elements important in and of themselves; they were also important because they facilitated the use of knowledge. When these elements were blocked, performance suffered. When they were unleashed, performance soared.

I've come to call these elements Faith, Fire, and Focus.

Faith has to do with our beliefs about ourselves and our beliefs about others.

Fire has to do with our energy, passion, motivation, and commitment.

Focus has to do with what we pay attention to and how we pay attention.

Faith, Fire, and Focus are what create engagement. They are how we get the 10X performance!

ENGAGED EMPLOYEE PROFILE

In their book, *Follow This Path*, Gallup Organization's Curt Coffman and Gabriel Gonzalez-Molina describe the attributes of the "engaged" employee—or one who, in my language, has optimized his/her Faith, Fire, and Focus on the job[1]:

- Use their talents every day.
- Show consistent levels of high performance.
- Exhibit natural innovation and drive for efficiency.
- Intentionally build supportive relationships.
- Are clear about the desired outcomes of their role.
- Are emotionally committed to what they do.
- Challenge purpose to achieve goals.
- Display high energy and enthusiasm.
- Never run out of things to do, but create positive things to act on.
- Broaden what they do and build on it.
- Show commitment to company, work group, and role.

Because the impact of these three elements is so significant, I have become increasingly convinced that *what separates high performers from everyone else is their Faith, Fire, and Focus.* And because the impact of interference on these elements is so profound, I have also become convinced that *reducing interference to Faith, Fire, and Focus is probably the least recognized but most effective way to improve performance.*

As we'll see in chapter 4, the good news is that there is a simple, scalable, replicable process that can make that happen.

A Model of Performance

Together, Knowledge, Faith, Fire, and Focus create what I call the "K3F" model of human performance.

If you look at this model as a wheel (page 18), Knowledge represents the rim. Faith, Fire, and Focus are like spokes supporting the wheel. The rim without the spokes or the spokes without the rim would render the wheel useless— as would a weakness of any of the four basic parts. Therefore, all four parts are vital to performance success.

As we observed in chapter 1, most performance improvement approaches pay attention primarily or even exclusively to the Knowledge component. Obviously, some basic Knowledge is essential. You'd find it hard to be a salesperson if you didn't know anything about your product, your customers, or the competition. You'd find it difficult to excel at tennis without knowing what a racket is, what a ball is, and the object and rules of the game. You'd find it

challenging to play a Mozart concerto without knowing the fundamentals of musical notes, rhythm, and dynamics.

However, it is Faith, Fire, and Focus that drive the quality of performance and performance improvement. This is what was released when interference was removed for the 10X girl. This is what enabled tennis champion Buster Mottram to move from ninetieth to nineteenth (or from good to world-class) in only six months. This is what creates results in organizations where people

- genuinely believe in the viability, competency, and purpose of the organization;
- are enthused about and engaged in their work;
- know what to pay attention to and are focused on the key objectives that would make the organization successful; and
- are able to fully execute on the Knowledge they already have.

When Faith, Fire, and Focus are released, extraordinary things happen. This is when possibility opens up.

So What's the Source of Faith, Fire, and Focus?

Faith, Fire, and Focus are innate in all of us. As toddlers, we believe in ourselves. We're excited about and interested in everything. We're totally focused on whatever's at hand. We're into everything. That's why Mom and Dad have to nail down everything in the house and cover the electrical sockets. We want to explore! Our insatiable curiosity is a manifestation of our Faith, Fire, and Focus.

> **I have no special gift. I am only passionately curious.**
>
> ALBERT EINSTEIN,
> Nobel Prize–
> winning theoretical
> physicist

Imagine what it was like when you were one year old. As you were exploring your world one day, you saw that Mom was holding a multicolored book. You had Faith—you believed that you could get that book. You had no reason to doubt it. You had Fire—you were excited about doing it. You had Focus—that was the only thing on your mind at the moment. So you went over and took that book away from her, and you explored it in every way you could. You looked at the bright colors. You listened to the noises it made as you banged it on the floor. As you handled it, you felt its smooth texture. And when you put it in your mouth, you discovered it tasted okay as well.

Quite quickly, however, you got bored with it. Then you noticed that one of Mom's friends was doodling on some paper with this slender, black, shiny thing, and you grabbed it in order to explore it. It felt good. It tasted okay when you put it in your mouth. But when you stuck it up your nose, it hurt. So you dropped it immediately and took Mom's book away again because that didn't hurt, it made good noise, and it felt okay. But you quickly got bored again with the book, and then you noticed that Mom's other friend had these long stringy things on his shoes that you could pull. So you yanked at them. But you couldn't get them to go anywhere, so you went over and grabbed at Mom's book yet again.

Now, what did Mom do the third time you tried to take her book away? In exasperation, she finally said sternly, "No! Go and play with something else. I'm trying to read this book." And that was probably the first emotionally scarring experience of your little life. Your most significant source of safety in the world was terrorizing you. Yet she still didn't shut down your curiosity. You went back. But this time you were in "watch-out" mode. You watched her face. You wanted to know—was she going to scold you or wasn't she? Because of this, you were hesitant as you reached for the book. Your concern was creating interference to your natural Faith, Fire, and Focus.

That's the moment in all our lives when learning starts to slow down. Once we go into watch-out mode, our defenses are up. We don't want another painful experience. So we're cautious. This is what happens in organizations when people's ideas are rejected and they get a "hand slapped," so to speak. They immediately go into watch-out mode. They become cautious. And others who see it happen or hear about it also go into watch-out mode, particularly when compensation issues are at stake.

As we grow out of the toddler stage, we have more and more experiences that increase this watch-out mode. Developmental psychologists tell us that we learn half of what we learn in our entire lives by the time we're five or six years old. When I ask people what they think happens that slows down learning so dramatically when we're five or six, they typically reply, "We go to school." School is where—if we haven't discovered it already—we learn that there's a "get approval" and a "not get approval" in this world. It's institutionalized in terms of passing or failing grades.

THE IMPACT OF WATCH-OUT MODE

In *Orbiting the Giant Hairball*, Gordon MacKenzie relates his experience working with students from a variety of elementary schools. He writes that whenever he would go into a first grade class and ask how many were artists, "*[e]n masse,* the children leapt from their chairs, arms waving wildly, eager hands trying to reach the ceiling. Every child was an artist."

In second grade, "[a]bout half the kids raised their hands, shoulder high, no higher. The raised hands were still." He concludes: "By the time I reached sixth grade, no more than one or two [raised their hands] and then only ever-so-slightly—*guardedly*—their eyes glancing from side to side uneasily, betraying a fear of being identified by the group as a 'closet artist.'"[2]

In addition to whatever comments children may hear from teachers or peers at school, what do they hear from us as parents that helps create this watch-out mode? When our six-year-old brings us a painting he/she has done, even if we have no idea what it's about, we say, "Oh, that's wonderful! You are so clever! What a fantastic job!" But when that child is eight, what are we more likely to say? "That's a great picture, but don't you think you should make that circle a bit more round?" And when that child is ten? "That's a horse? It doesn't look like a horse to me."

As we mature, we become involved in what we see as win-lose competition—in sports, in academics, in dating—sometimes even for attention and recognition in the family. We go to work, where organizations—by their very nature—put us in watch-out mode. Little by little, our Focus shifts from exploring and learning to avoiding and defending. Our Faith is shaken. Our Fire is dimmed.

> **Every child is an artist. The problem is how to remain an artist once we grow up.**
>
> PABLO PICASSO,
> Spanish painter,
> draftsman, and
> sculptor

Being Told What to Do

Another thing that happens during our toddler and preschool years is that we start to develop language skills. As a result, an increasing number of people in our lives—parents, then teachers, then athletic coaches, then bosses and others—use language as a tool to *tell* us what they think we should do and how they think we should do it . . . in other words, to try to communicate Knowledge to us.

Can you imagine what it would have been like if your parents had tried to teach you to walk in the same way they tried to teach you to play baseball or some other sport? "Okay, now I want you to stand with your weight evenly on both feet. Bend your knees. Not that much—just a little. Okay, now pick up your right leg. No! Not that far. Oops, you fell over, didn't you? Okay, get up. We're going to try this again. Now this time, pay attention. Concentrate!" Your parents probably didn't do that. They knew you couldn't understand their instructions at that age. So they put you in a safe environment, let you experiment on your own so that you could learn for yourself what did and didn't work, and were totally optimistic and supportive of your efforts. "That was awesome! You are so smart! I love you!" When you fell down, they helped you up and let you try—and fall—again. And why did they do that? Because they instinctively knew how to maximize your learning when you were a child. They created a learning environment that was safe—emotionally and physically—and then they relied on your inherent Faith, Fire, and Focus as well as feedback from your own experience to help you learn.

What a contrast to the environments in many organizations today. And what a difference in results. Most of the time people's attempts to tell us what to do are well intended. And certainly we need to have Knowledge of critical variables in any area of performance we choose to pursue. But the amount of Knowledge we are given and the way in which most of it is given shifts our Focus from exploring and learning to trying to remember and follow the instructions of others to do things "right." As a result, our Faith in our own learning capacity dwindles even further, and our Fire continues to dim.

> **The great man is he who does not lose his child-heart.**
>
> MENCIUS,
> ancient Chinese
> philosopher

Unblocking Faith, Fire, and Focus

As long as Faith, Fire, and Focus are diminished or blocked, no amount of effort—on the part of the coach or the performer—will create anything near top performance. But when these elements are released, high performance comes naturally and quickly, and improvement far exceeds anything the coach could drive on his/her own. This is why effective coaches will pay at least as much attention to the Faith, Fire, and Focus of the individual as they do to Knowledge or even to performance. They learn to empower through Faith, Fire, and Focus rather than disempower with interference.

I'd like to share with you an example of an organization that seems to me to have been designed from the beginning to reduce the interference that blocks Faith, Fire, and Focus. Nestled in the green fields of Suffolk, England, is the campus of an unusual—and somewhat controversial—private boarding school called Summerhill. It was founded in 1921 by A. S. Neill, a man later recognized as one of the twelve greatest educators of the past millennium.[3] What makes Summerhill unique is that students and faculty run it together as a "community of equals." Rigorous classes are held at regularly scheduled times, but children are free to attend—or not—as they choose. Emphasis is placed on the importance of the freedom of a student to "play"—to do whatever interests him or her—and students participate equally with teachers in meetings in which all decisions are made. Referring to Summerhill, A. S. Neill said:

> We set out to make a school in which we should allow children freedom to be themselves . . . We have been called brave, but it did not require courage. All it required was what we had—a complete belief in the child as a good,

not an evil, being. Since 1921 this belief in the goodness of the child has never wavered; it rather has become a final faith."[4]

Because of its unusual philosophy, Summerhill has been subjected to an inordinate number of inspections over the years, and in 1999, a division of the British government took steps to shut the school down. However, an independent inquiry found that although children did spend a good deal of time at play (particularly at first), Summerhill students had better than average results in public exams, and most went on to attain college degrees and satisfying careers. Many expressed gratitude for what Summerhill had done for them, particularly in the areas of self-confidence, interpersonal skills, caring about and respect for others, a sense of personal responsibility, and the ability to make their own decisions. These findings were especially impressive considering that a number of these students had previously been failing academically in the state schooling environment.[5] One former student said, "I learned more at Summerhill in my one year of being able to attend what subjects I wanted and as many classes as interested me than I did in four years of US high school." Another said: "We were treated like individuals, like intelligent and responsible human beings. We were respected and encouraged to be ethical and responsible. We learned how to live in a group in a sane way."[6]

> **Education is not filling a bucket, but lighting a fire.**
>
> **WILLIAM BUTLER YEATS**, Irish poet and dramatist

My reason for sharing this information about Summerhill is neither to praise nor condemn the school or its philosophy. It's merely to give context for the following observation. As parents and/or educators, many of us are incredulous to think that children left to their own initiative in a learning environment would actually choose to pursue academic and social excellence and that they would often do it faster and more enthusiastically than their peers in traditional compulsory education. More broadly, as managers, leaders, coaches, or parents, we're incredulous to think (or more likely, it never even occurs to us to think) that without our excessive instructing, regulating, controlling, directing, and intervening, people might actually be able to perform with greater confidence, more enthusiasm, and more effective focus.

Perhaps we would do well to pay more attention to what's blocking Faith,

Fire, and Focus in our organizations, performers, families, and teams—and to think about what might happen if those things were removed. To explore the possibilities, let's take a deeper look at each of these elements of high performance.

Faith

Faith is about belief. And put simply, belief drives behavior. Whether we believe we're intelligent or stupid, lovable or unlovable, in charge of our lives or victims without choice, those beliefs drive what we do. And because what we *do* leads to the *results* we get in our lives, beliefs also drive results. For example, if I'm giving a presentation and I genuinely believe that I'm well prepared and can communicate my thoughts and ideas effectively, I'll be relaxed, enthusiastic, and personable during the presentation. But if I believe I'm not adequately prepared or if I'm worried about my ability to express myself or the audience's possibly negative reaction, I'll be nervous, and my fear about the audience's response will become a self-fulfilling prophecy. As a result, my chances of communicating and influencing effectively will be diminished.

> **What great thing would you attempt if you knew you couldn't fail?**
>
> DR. ROBERT H. SCHULLER, American minister and author

Or if I'm playing tennis, and I believe I can return my opponent's serve, I'll be on my toes, attention focused, hunting for the ball, and I'll have a good chance of returning the serve. If I don't believe I can return the serve, I'll be on my heels, shoulders slumping, thinking negative, self-defeating thoughts and my chances of success will be significantly reduced.

The Faith that seems to improve performance the most is believing "I can learn." It's not "I believe I can win Wimbledon a week after I take my first tennis lesson." It's "I believe I have the capacity to learn and improve at tennis." Or "I believe I have the capacity to become a better musician . . . or manager . . . or teacher . . . or parent."

MIND-SET RESEARCH

Stanford psychologist Carol Dweck has done extensive research showing the difference between people who believe that ability is something people are born with and those who believe it can be developed. (This latter perspective reflects Faith in our ability to learn, or in what we could call the "learner within.")

Those who believe ability is inherent typically believe that success should come easily. They're not motivated to practice. They see failure as a lack of ability and are easily discouraged. On the other hand, those who see ability as something that can be developed believe that success is a result of effort. They're motivated—not discouraged—by failure. They see themselves as learners and problem solvers, and if one solution doesn't work, they're ready to try another.

Dweck's research also reveals a difference between those who have "performance" goals and those who have "learning" goals—and a difference in the results. She says, "Students for whom performance is paramount want to look smart even if it means not learning a thing in the process. For them, each task is a challenge to their self-image, and each setback becomes a personal threat. So they pursue only activities at which they're sure to shine—and avoid the sorts of experiences necessary to grow and flourish in any endeavor. Students with learning goals, on the other hand, take necessary risks and don't worry about failure because each mistake becomes a chance to learn."

In further affirmation of the learner within, Dweck concludes that "praising children for intelligence, rather than for effort, sap[s] their motivation" (or Fire). She also affirms that people can change their mind-sets (or their Faith) and therefore improve their performance.[7]

The absence of Faith could be described as insecurity. It's fear and self-doubt. It's what we feel when we don't know how to deal with the negative, critical voices inside our own heads—when we distort, magnify, or imagine the criticism or negative judgment of others . . . when we feel afraid of not doing things the "right" way . . . when we live out of worry over the past or anxiety over the future . . . when we get stuck in the "stories" we tell about ourselves: "I'll never get promoted." "I get too nervous to make good presentations." "I can't do strategy." "I'm a slow learner." "I'm not a people person." "I'm shy."

Sometimes these stories begin with a set of events that get quickly exaggerated or distorted and take on expanded meaning along the way. On the first hole of the golf course, for example, if you hit a "slice" (a shot where the ball curves frustratingly to the right), you might say, "Oh, *there is* a slice." If you do it again on the fourth hole, you might expand your judgment to say, *"I sliced."* If you repeat the shot on the eighth hole, you might take it even further: *"I have* a slice." If you do it again on the tenth hole, you say, *"I am* a slicer." And if you three putt on the seventeenth hole, you might decide, *"I am* a bad golfer." And if your spouse phones you when you're on the eighteenth tee and says, "Where are you? Why aren't you home for dinner?" you might even decide you're not a good husband/wife—or even a good person—either.

Or maybe you do it at the office. You're asked to speak at a team meeting. You don't intend to be funny, but people laugh at what you say. You think, "Well, I guess *that didn't* come across very clearly." The next time you try to explain something to a team member, he tells you you're wrong; you don't understand. You think, "I guess *I don't* communicate clearly." When you present a report and a lot of people have questions, you think, *"I am* not a clear speaker." When the boss calls you in to clarify something you said in a meeting, you think, *"I am* not very good at my job." And when your companion storms out of the house because of something you said, you stoically determine that you're never going to open your mouth again.

Though we usually don't even recognize it, the limiting stories we tell about ourselves are at play all the time. They impact our performance. They narrow our perception of our possibilities. They act as a filter through which we interpret the events of our lives. Because I was asthmatic as a child, I was constantly being told, "You can't do what other people can do. It's okay to not go swimming. It's okay to come off the soccer field in the middle of the game." So that became my story, my belief system through which everything got filtered. When I would try to run and get a little out of breath, a little voice in my head would begin to say, "Here we go. This is what they're talking about." And I would start to tense up and tell myself, "Wow! It's getting harder to breathe." So those thoughts would become a self-fulfilling prophecy—*even after my condition improved!* A real breakthrough came for me when the Walkman (a battery-powered personal stereo with headphones) was invented, and I began to run while wearing one. For the first time in my life, I could go five miles without stopping. Because my mind was focused on something other than those inner voices, the voices began to fade, and suddenly I found myself doing more than I'd ever done before—more than I had thought I could ever do. Transcending the grip of that story made a huge difference in my belief about what was possible and in my ability to perform.

I have since learned that having the equivalent of a Walkman on at work or in other situations can create similar results. It enables a person to Focus exclusively on the key beliefs and goals that lead to high performance instead of getting bogged down by interference and stories that limit performance. It releases Faith and Fire. We'll talk about the process that helps create that kind of Focus in chapter 4.

When we *don't* transcend our stories we get stuck in them, and instead of fully experiencing and learning from the present, we're constantly reliving our experience of the past. Some time ago, I was traveling on a plane from Stockholm to London. A woman sat beside me, and the moment the plane began to move, she grabbed my arm with such vigor I thought she was going to tear it off. She was anxious, nervous, and clearly afraid. After a short time in the air, she seemed to calm down a bit, but when we started to land she became extremely anxious again. As we talked, I discovered she had been through a frightening incident on an airplane some time before, and that experience had affected her response to every flight she'd been on since. What was causing this woman's mental and emotional distress on our flight was not what was actually happening, but what she imagined *might* happen. She was stuck in a story from the past, and it was filtering her experience of the present.

One of the most debilitating stories we get stuck in is the one that denies possibility: "It can't be done." When people aren't getting results in their lives or in their teams, their families, or their organizations, they almost always have a story as to why they aren't getting results. A very common story is "We don't have enough Knowledge." Breakthroughs don't come until these stories change. Creating change is hard because we tend to think that what we say about something is the truth—when, in reality, it's only our *perception* of the truth. Recognizing our ability to change that perception is at the heart of developing the kind of Faith that leads to top performance.

The bottom line is that we choose our beliefs, our beliefs determine our actions, and our actions determine the results. To the degree to which we choose different beliefs and therefore change the stories we tell about ourselves—or our employees, or our organization, or our students, or our spouse, or our children—we change the ability to perform.

Fire

Fire is about energy and passion. It's manifested in the commitment we often see expressed in people or companies that do great and inspiring things—not only Nobel Prize winners such as Muhammad Yunus, Nelson Mandela, and Mother Teresa or great performers and athletes such as Luciano Pavarotti, Yo-Yo Ma, and Tiger Woods but also volunteers who spend hundreds of hours running literacy centers, staffing soup kitchens, and providing medical care for people in third world countries; teachers who devote their off-duty time to tutor kids in troubled inner-city areas; elementary school students who raise money for the victims of earthquakes and tsunamis; parents who selflessly devote the best of their time, energy, and resources to nurturing and raising happy, well-adjusted children. It's the motivation that releases adrenalin and enables people to transcend their normal abilities—overcoming challenges, breaking world records, doing seemingly impossible things such as lifting cars off of loved ones trapped in accidents.

THE HEART OF CHANGE

In their book *The Heart of Change,* Harvard Business professor John Kotter and Deloitte Consulting principal Dan Cohen assert that "[c]hanging behavior is less a matter of giving people analysis to influence their thoughts than helping them to see a truth to influence their feelings. Both thinking and feelings are essential, and both are found in successful organizations, but the heart of change is in the emotions. The flow of see-feel-change is more powerful than that of analysis-think-change."[8]

One of the most inspirational examples to me of how Fire affects performance is a man named Dick Hoyt. Forty-three years ago, Dick's infant son, Rick, was strangled by his umbilical cord during birth, cutting off the oxygen supply to his brain. Dick and his wife were told that Rick would be severely handicapped—mentally and physically—for the rest of his life, and he should be put in an institution. Instead, the Hoyts brought him home. When he was eleven, they asked the engineering department of a nearby university to devise a way to help him communicate. They were told it couldn't be done because there was nothing going on in Rick's brain. But when Dick told them to tell Rick a joke—and Rick laughed—they changed their minds. They created a computer that enabled him to control the cursor by touching a switch with the side of his head. Through the computer, Rick communicated to his dad that he wanted to participate in a charity run. So Dick, "a self-described 'porker' who never ran more than a mile at a time,"[9] ran and pushed his son in a wheelchair for five miles. Rick typed on his computer: "Dad, when we were running, it felt like I wasn't disabled anymore!"[10]

Those words ignited a passion in Dick. He was determined to do whatever it took to inspire that feeling in his son. He worked hard to get in shape and eventually qualified to run with Rick in marathons and even Ironman triathlons, which included 2.4 miles of swimming (with Rick being pulled in a dingy roped to Dick's waist), 112 miles of bicycling (with Rick on a seat on the handlebars), and 26.2 miles of running (with Dick pushing Rick in a wheelchair). To date, Dick (now sixty-five) and Rick (forty-three) have participated in 24 Boston Marathons and 212 triathlons, including 4 fifteen-hour Ironmans. Their best time in the Boston Marathon was two hours, forty minutes—only thirty-five minutes off the world record for all participants.

> **Man is so made that when anything fires his soul, impossibilities vanish.**
>
> **JEAN DE LA FONTAINE,**
> French poet

The Fire of Dick Hoyt's love for his son released the Faith that enabled him to do things he never thought he could do. In the same way, Fire in the organization, team, classroom, or family also unleashes Faith that impels people to perform well beyond what they think they can do.

Fire shows itself in different ways in different people. While I've known top salespeople who fit the stereotype of being dynamic, charismatic, and outgoing, I've known others who have been quiet and reserved but have beat the socks off the competition with their drive and passion for hard work.

The absence of Fire could be described as indifference. It's low motivation, low energy, lack of commitment. You see it in people who aren't clear on their highest priorities in life or whose lives are not aligned to those priorities. You see it in people who are feeling overwhelmed, overburdened, or burned out. You see it in people whose lives have taken an unexpected turn that they haven't accepted or figured out how to deal with. There is a powerful relationship between Faith and Fire. Once people get out of their unproductive stories and begin to see possibility (Faith), their Fire grows.

Focus

Focus is about directed attention or concentration. It's what leads to the quiet mind and sense of effortlessness we feel when we do things well. It's what gives us the ability to be in "the here and now," paying full attention to the task at hand, uninterrupted by other distractions. A high degree of Focus channels energy and ability to accomplish tasks and meet challenges in extraordinary ways. Not only is it a critical element of performance; it's also a critical element of practice. As legendary American football coach Vince Lombardi said, "Practice does not make perfect. Only perfect practice makes perfect." By creating appropriate Focus during practice, a performer can actually reduce the practice time necessary to create the habits needed for top performance.

Over the years, I've become convinced that Focus is the defining difference in human performance. It's what enables successful CEOs such as Louis Gerstner (IBM) and Herb Kelleher (Southwest Airlines) to concentrate collective effort on a few key goals and turn troubled corporations around. It's what separates Tiger Woods's performance on the golf course from that of every other golfer on the PGA Tour, especially when the pressure is on. It's what changes people's Faith (their belief about what they can do), their Fire (their energy for doing it), and their acquisition and use of Knowledge.

THE TOP PERFORMANCE DIFFERENCE

On the 2007 PGA tour, the difference in scoring average between the #1 golfer (Tiger Woods) and #2 (Jeff Overton) was only 1.5 strokes per round. But while Tiger took home approximately $10.8 million in prize money, Overton earned only a little over $1 million. In addition, Tiger took home more than $80 million from endorsements.

We've all experienced the power of Focus—when we become so absorbed in a project that we're not even aware of what's going on around us; when we get so caught up in the emotion of a piece of music we're playing that we don't even think about technique or notes; when we're having such a good time with our best friend or reading a book or watching a movie that we lose all track of time. This is the kind of Focus that manifests itself in high performance. When I was working with Welsh golfer David Llewellyn, he shot the

European tour record for the lowest round of golf in any professional event (sixty). But he was so into the experience of the moment that he had no idea he'd done it until after the round was over!

We also know what it's like when we get distracted and our Focus shifts to something other than what's critical—when we forget what we started to say; when we inadvertently let things fall through the cracks; when we miss the service return in tennis because we're distracted by the crowd instead of keeping our eye on the ball.

> **Your ability to divert your attention from activities of lower value to activities of higher value is central to everything you accomplish in life.**
>
> BRIAN TRACY,
> business author
> and speaker

Clearly, Focus is a powerful tool for removing distractions, and it is vital to high performance on every level. Several years ago, I met with the managing director of a product design and manufacturing business in China to help him work on using Focus to improve his tennis game. As we worked together, this man became excited about his success on the court, but he became even more excited about the possibility of applying the principle of Focus in his business. When he returned to the factory, he began to work on shifting the Focus of the Chinese workers from "whether some obscure measurement on the back of a drawer was two microns off" to "the three things that really made the greatest difference to the American consumer—look, feel and function." He worked with his employees to create a program in which every item the company produced was rated on those three things. The result? In his words:

In 2004, out of millions of dollars of business, we had somewhere around eight to nine percent defective product. With the prioritized focus simply on looks, feel and function, by 2006 we had reduced that figure to less than one percent. As you can imagine, that had a huge impact on our profit margin. But it also had a huge impact on morale as well. People began to realize that they were more capable, more powerful than they had previously thought. The principle of focused attention turned out to be the simple answer to a huge problem.

FOCUS AND EXECUTION

In *What Leaders Really Do,* Harvard Business School professor John Kotter observes that general managers noted for getting results have these things in common—they focus totally on a limited agenda of clear core objectives, and they keep their people constantly and measurably moving forward on those objectives.[11]

In *Execution: The Discipline of Getting Things Done,* former CEO of Honeywell International Larry Bossidy and business advisor Ram Charan observe: "A leader who says 'I've got ten priorities' doesn't know what he's talking about—he doesn't know himself what the most important things are. You've got to have these few, clearly realistic goals and priorities, which will influence the overall performance of the company."[12]

One of the primary reasons Focus is so foundational to high performance is because it clears our minds and therefore increases the quality of feedback from our own experience. Without feedback, we have no way to know whether we're actually doing what we think we're doing or getting the results we think we're getting. Feedback is data, and the more accurate data we have to work with, the faster we can learn.

The absence of Focus could be described as inconsistency. It's what causes golfers to land the ball on the green on one hole and in the water the next. It's what causes us to tell our kids "no" one day and "yes" the next, creating confusion and encouraging them to continually test the limits. It's what causes teams and organizations to keep switching from one strategy to another. It's what makes team meetings interminably long and repetitive and therefore costly in terms of time, frustration, and ultimately, money.

As we'll see in the following chapters, controlling Focus is the most effective way to release Faith and Fire. When Focus draws our attention to that which is specific and doable, it reduces interference. It quiets the mind. It changes our belief and therefore our confidence in our ability to do, which in turn releases more energy, passion, and excitement about doing.

All Three Are Necessary

Faith, Fire, and Focus are all necessary for top performance. And this is true whether you're dealing with individual performance (as a manager, leader, athlete, parent, teacher, etc.), team performance (in a work team, athletic team, or even in a marriage or family), organizational performance, or your own performance as a "coach" in helping others.

It's possible to have Faith, Fire, and Focus that don't lead to high performance if your beliefs are limiting, your energy is negative, or you're focused on the wrong things. But for the purpose of this book, we're talking about the positive dimensions of these elements that *do* lead to high performance—belief in our ability to learn and to do, energy and excitement about doing, and attention to the critical variables that result in performance improvement. In that context, with Faith and Fire, but no Focus, people believe in themselves and have energy and commitment but are inconsistent in their ability to perform. With Faith and Focus, but no Fire, people are confident and stay on task but really don't care about what they're doing and won't commit (which is the number one issue in today's workforce). With Fire and Focus, but no Faith, people are passionate about what they do and stay on task but are insecure and always doubt themselves.

PERFORMANCE	
High	**Low**
Faith Belief in one's ability to learn/adapt	**Insecurity** Fear and self-doubt
Fire Passion, energy, commitment	**Indifference** Apathy, lack of interest, compliance
Focus Attention, concentration	**Inconsistency** Distracted/interrupted effort, irregularity in performance

As I mentioned at the beginning of this chapter, Faith, Fire, and Focus—together with Knowledge—create a model of human performance. This K3F model provides a useful lens through which we can understand, evaluate, and create change in our own performance. As we'll see in chapters 5 and 6, it can also help us coach others to improved performance. And as we'll discuss in chapter 7, the model gives us a lens through which we can better understand and improve organizational performance as well.

The Bottom Line

Whatever our capacity, we have a greater chance of fulfilling it when

- we believe that we can learn and do better (Faith);
- we are excited about learning and doing (Fire); and
- we pay attention in a way that will quiet our minds (Focus).

The good news is that because Faith, Fire, and Focus are innate, we have the ability to renew the Faith, rekindle the Fire, and re-create the Focus we were born with and that are so vital to high performance. That happens as we get rid of the interference that blocks these natural, inherent human gifts.

Reflective Questions

- Take a look at your organization or your family. What evidence do you see of people in watch-out mode? What effect do you think this is having on performance and/or possibility?

- What stories are you telling about yourself that are limiting your own performance? What stories are you telling about others that might be limiting theirs?

- To what extent do you feel your Faith, your Fire, and your Focus are each currently engaged:
  — In your personal life?
  — In your professional life?
  — In a chosen area of interest (sports, music, etc.)?

- What difference might it make if you were able to tap more fully into your Faith, Fire, and Focus?

- Think about how Faith, Fire, and Focus may be affecting the lives or performance of others—coworkers, spouse, children, students, athletes, or others? What might be different about the performance of these people if they were able to more fully tap into their Faith, Fire, and Focus?

Chapter 2: For an exercise that will help you
TAKE A CLOSER LOOK AT THE IMPACT
OF KNOWLEDGE, FAITH, FIRE,
AND FOCUS ON YOUR PERFORMANCE
Access the online community at
Alan-Fine.com

CHAPTER THREE

Getting Rid of Interference

Focus is what distracts us from whatever is distracting us.

TIMOTHY GALLWEY,
Inner Game creator and author

For the first time in my life, I really thought I was going to die. I wanted to scream. I wanted to turn around and go back. I wanted to be anywhere other than where I was—thirty feet out on a long, narrow ridge with what appeared to be a thousand-foot drop onto broken rocks on the left and a five-hundred-foot drop onto a glacier on the right . . . roped together with four other people . . . with no way to turn around and go back.

It was the summer of 1986. Chris Bonington—a well-known Everest climber from the UK—had asked if I would help facilitate a leadership program he was running for some executives from Apple Computer in Europe. The event was centered around climbing Mont Blanc, the highest mountain in Europe. Given that the highest peak I'd ever climbed was the hill to my local pub, I was a bit nervous about it. But I was so flattered by the invitation from Chris that I couldn't say no.

We spent the first two days acclimating and training—learning things such as how to put on crampons, how to use an ice ax to break our fall if we slipped, and what to do if another team member began to fall. On the third day, we were to train on l'Aiguille du Midi—a smaller peak—as part of our preparation. To get there, we had to ride part of the way to the peak in a tram, which let us out in a cave. There, instead of turning right and going to the restaurant where the tourists go, we turned left and went through the tunnel where the climbers go. We put on very dark sunglasses so that we wouldn't go snow-blind when we exited the cave. With the glasses on, it was difficult to see much at all as we headed to the exit. Five of us, all roped together, groped our way out of the tunnel and onto the ridge. It took several seconds for my eyes to adjust to the light, so we'd already gone about twenty or thirty paces before I was able to clearly see where I was. When I did see, my stomach lurched and my legs locked. I knew I was going to fall, and not only would I die; I would take everyone else with me. I was paralyzed with fear!

InterFEARence

What I experienced that day on l'Aiguille du Midi was a form of interference—or perhaps more appropriately in this case, interFEARence. And that interFEARence completely blocked my Faith. (I did not believe I could take one more step.) It extinguished my Fire. (I had NO desire to continue this perilous adventure.) It consumed my Focus. (My attention was riveted on the terror I was experiencing and my absolute conviction that my demise was imminent.)

Though perhaps not as dramatically, to one degree or another interference affects our Faith, Fire, and Focus—and our performance—nearly every day. Some of this interference is *external*. It comes from things that are mostly outside our direct control. In the marketplace it might be the economy, new technology, or increased competition. On the tennis court it might be the wind, the sun, the court surface, or an opponent. At home it could be economics, the media, or the demands and expectations of family members and others. Onstage it might be the lights, another performer's missed cue, the rustling of programs in the audience, or the sound of a siren outside the theater. In many situations it's judgmental communication—both verbal and nonverbal—from other people.

But much of the interference that affects our performance is *internal*. A good deal of it comes from our response to external interference. It's reflected in the stories we tell about ourselves, the way we approach situations in watch-out mode, the way we worry about the past or the future or think of all the things we should be doing instead of focusing on the present. It's manifest in the conversations we have with what I call the "eight-hundred-pound gorillas inside our heads"—the

> There are many ways of allowing your thinking to get in the way of your performance and learning, but they all amount to conversations you are having with yourself within your own head.
>
> TIMOTHY GALLWEY, *Inner Game* creator and author

internal dialogue that goes: "You have to do this the 'right' way." "Don't screw this up!" "You're stupid." "You're inadequate." "You can't do this!" "Can't you do anything right?" "What will others say?"

We all have our gorillas—CEOs, salespeople, athletes, parents, kids, beginners, professionals, you, me . . . it doesn't matter; no one is exempt. And it's the noisy chatter of these gorillas—not busyness—that creates internal interference. In fact, it's possible to be *very* busy and still have the quiet mind necessary for top performance, as long as you're focused.

As I experienced that day on l'Aiguille du Midi . . . and as an eleven-year-old boy facing the school jock in the tennis finals . . . and at many other times in my life, most internal interference comes from fear—not only fear of physical harm but, more commonly, fear of being judged, making a fool of myself, being rejected, or failing.

The problem is compounded because our minds tend to exaggerate what we're afraid of. Take a look at the two illustrations below. The left shows a kind of external interference on the golf course that most of us would fear—a water hazard. The very presence of a water hazard causes us to "choke." But in almost every golfer's mind, water increases the force of gravity on golf balls by a hundredfold! We become afraid we're going to hit the ball in the water and lose a shot—and a three-dollar ball as well. And because of our fear, our minds make the hazard seem more challenging than it actually is (at right).

Issues such as staff fluctuations, reorganizations, changing skill requirements, new technologies, the challenge to do more with less, information overload, cultural diversity, layoffs, and performance appraisals create the same kind of interference in the organization that the water hazard does on the golf course. And this significantly affects organizational performance. For example, a salesperson who's given a target with a 50 percent increase over last year or a project manager who's told the launch date has been moved up by three months typically sees the challenge as much larger than it actually is. The immediate reaction is, "This can't be done!" When people throughout the organization respond in this way, the collective impact keeps the organization from learning and performing at its highest level.

FEAR IN THE WORKPLACE

In their book *Driving Fear Out of the Workplace: Creating the High-Trust, High-Performance Organization,* Kathleen Ryan and Daniel Oestreich identify other specific concerns that create interFEARence for many.

- Having one's credibility questioned
- Being left out of decision making
- Being criticized in front of others
- Not getting information necessary to succeed
- Having a key assignment given to someone else
- Having disagreements that might lead to damaged relationships
- Getting stuck in a dead-end job
- Not getting deserved recognition
- Not being seen as a team player
- Having suggestions ignored or misinterpreted as criticisms
- Receiving poor performance ratings
- Getting fired[1]

So how do we get rid of the interference? Usually, we can't change the external interference. It's just the way things are. As my teenage son so aptly says, we need to "just deal with it!" However, by reducing the internal interference, we can free ourselves and/or others to get at higher performance. And the simplest and most accessible way to get rid of internal interference is through Focus—through changing *what* we pay attention to and *how* we pay attention.

THE ART OF POSSIBILITY

In teaching classes at the New England Conservatory of Music, Boston Philharmonic Orchestra conductor Benjamin Zander noticed that the biggest inhibitor of performance improvement in his classes was fear associated with grades. So he decided to simply remove that interFEARence.

At the beginning of the year, he announced that all students would automatically receive an A for the entire year if they would fulfill one requirement within the next two weeks. They simply had to write a letter as though they were writing at the end of the year, explaining in detail what they had done to receive their A. They had to share their feelings, insights, and accomplishments as though they had already occurred and describe the person they had become.

A young Korean flute player wrote the following:

I received my grade A because I worked hard and thought hard about myself taking your class, and the result was absolutely tremendous. I became a new person. I used to be so negative person for almost everything even before trying. Now I find myself happier person than before. I couldn't accept my mistakes about a year ago, and after every mistake I blamed myself, but now, I enjoy making mistakes and I really learn from these mistakes. In my playing I have more depth than before. I used to play just notes, but, now, I found out about the real meaning of every pieces, and I could play with more imagination. Also I found out my value. I found myself so special person, because I found out that if I believe myself I can do everything. Thank you for all the lessons and lectures because that made me realize how important person I am and also the clear reason why I play music.

Just think about the difference between teaching a typical student who is anxious about grades and focused on jumping through the hoops and pleasing the instructor versus teaching an A student who is focused on positive learning outcomes such as these. The impact can be transformational. In the words of Ben Zander, "Small wonder that I approach each class with the greatest eagerness, for this is a class consisting entirely of A students and what is more delightful than spending an afternoon among the stars?"[2]

Creating Focused Attention

After a lifetime of studying human performance, Claremont Graduate University professor Mihaly Csikszentmihalyi suggested that we all perform best when there is a balance between our perception of the challenge we are facing and our perception of the skill we have to meet the challenge. In other words, we need to have enough challenge to keep us excited, but not so much that it overwhelms or discourages us. According to Csikszentmihalyi, this is when we're most likely to get into a state of "flow"—a state where we're focused, fully engaged, and intrinsically motivated. In this state, we process things faster, learn faster, and are often not even aware of time or space. It's in this state that whatever we're doing seems almost effortless.[3]

THE FLOW EXPERIENCE

Below is a diagram showing the ideal balance between challenge and capacity that results in flow.

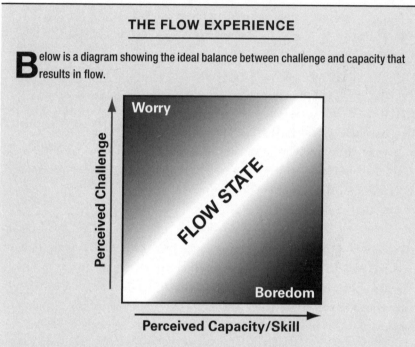

Adapted from "Beyond Boredom & Anxiety"
by Mihaly Csikszentmihalyi

People's descriptions of being in a flow state universally reflect a sense of intense focus and engagement.

From a dancer: *"Your concentration is very complete. Your mind isn't wandering, you are not thinking of something else; you are totally involved in what you are doing . . . Your energy is flowing very smoothly. You feel relaxed, comfortable, and energetic."*

From a rock climber: *"You are so involved in what you are doing [that] you aren't thinking of yourself as separate from the immediate activity . . . You don't see yourself as separate from what you are doing."*

From a chess player: *"[T]he concentration is like breathing—you never think of it. The roof could fall in and, if it missed you, you would be unaware of it."*[4]

Flow involves a deep Focus on what the performer perceives as a doable task—a focus that, by its very nature, eliminates interference. This, in and of itself, is a powerful performance idea for managers and leaders. Often we push people out of flow simply by overwhelming them with too much too frequently repeated Knowledge or by the way we cascade goals or assign tasks. Something as simple as tying a goal to compensation, particularly in a tight economy, can create huge interference for the employee who's struggling to support a family and make ends meet. It stands to reason that if we can chunk down the challenge into tasks that feel doable and then create a singular Focus on one or more critical variables of the task, we're far more likely to create the flow state that creates high performance. This is the kind of Focus I'm referring to when I talk about "changing what you pay attention to and how you pay attention."

> **Because of the total demand on psychic energy, a person in flow is completely focused. There is no space in consciousness for distracting thoughts, or irrelevant feelings.**[5]
>
> MIHALY CSIKSZENTMIHALYI, psychology professor and architect of the notion of flow

Let me share an example. The following conversation is adapted from an experience I had helping a man named Jim to hit a backhand in tennis. In most situations such as this, interference can be created by many things, including a coach's instructions (or an athlete's efforts to recall the coach's instructions), which keep the performer from focusing on the experience of the moment. As you read this dialogue, watch how chunking down the challenge helps Jim create Focus, remove interference, and improve his performance on the court. And notice what happens to his Faith and Fire along the way.

Alan: So Jim, we've got ten minutes to work on your tennis. What would you like out of the ten minutes?

Jim: I'd like to be able to hit a backhand.

Alan: Now what do you mean by hit a backhand?

Jim: [*laughing*] In the court.

Alan: Like anywhere on the other side of the net. Is that what you mean?

Jim: No, I'd really like to hit it on this side of the court [*indicating the opposite side across the net*] in the lines.

Alan: Okay, so that side of the court, over the net, within those lines on the green. And how often would you have to do that?

Jim: Half the time.

Alan: Like five times out of ten?

Jim: Right.

Alan: Okay, how often do you think you can do it at the moment?

Jim: Maybe two or three.

Alan: So, we're talking about a sixty-six percent improvement.

Jim: Yes.

Alan: Does that sound realistic to you?

Jim: Sure.

Alan: Okay. So, if we could help you to knock five out of ten backhands into that half of the court, would that be worthwhile?

Jim: It'd be great.

Alan: Okay. What I'd like to do is throw you some balls, and let's see if you can really do three out of ten. [*I toss Jim ten balls. Two of them land where he wants them to go.*]

Alan: So what's your sense of how many you can do?

Jim: [*laughing*] Two or three.

Alan: Okay. So is five out of ten still realistic?

Jim: If you're a good coach!

Alan: [*laughing*] Okay. So, seriously . . .

Jim: Yeah, I'd love to do that.

Alan: When you were playing those shots, what did you notice? What got your attention?

Jim: That I didn't have any confidence in my backhand.

Alan: How do you know that? How do you experience you're not confident?

Jim: I'm just not watching the ball.

Alan: I'll throw you some more and just let me know what you are aware of that tells you you're not confident.

Jim: [*after hitting a few more balls*] Well, I'm *seeing* the ball.

Alan: Okay. So, what are you *actually* seeing? Give me more detail about that.

Jim: [*continuing to hit more balls and commenting after each hit*] Well, I can see the line on it.

Alan: All right, tell me more about the line.

Jim: The line was moving slow.

Alan: Okay. How about this one?

Jim: That was fast.

Alan: This one?

Jim: That was slower.

Alan: Okay. Now when you say they're fast, are they equally fast each time, or does it vary?

Jim: They vary a little, but it's hard to tell.

Alan: Could you put it on a scale where, say, "one" is slow and "five" is fast?

Jim: Sure. [*continuing to hit balls and comment*] That was a five. [*pause*] That was a seven.

Alan: Okay.

Jim: That was an eight. [*pause*] That was a ten! [*by this time, most of the balls are landing where Jim wanted them to land*]

Alan: All right. [*I stop throwing the balls*] Now just let me check something with you, Jim. What's your sense of how we're doing?

Jim: [*with a huge grin*] I'm doing a *lot* better.

Alan: Do you know how many went in?

Jim: I think more than five.

Alan: Yeah, I think so, too. My sense is there are seven or eight out of ten going in.

Jim   That's great!

Alan: Is that what you wanted?

Jim: No—it's more! Thanks!

When a tennis player tries to improve, what typically goes through his/ her mind are thoughts such as the following: "Change your grip." "Get your feet right." "Prepare early." "Swing smoothly." Jim already knows these things are important. The reason he's not doing them is not that he doesn't know; it's that he's so busy trying to remember all the things he thinks he needs to do to handle this difficult challenge that he's not tracking where the ball *is* or accurately sensing what his body is doing.

As we chunk down the challenge, Jim begins to shift his Focus to *something he thinks he can do* (i.e., report back to me what he's noticing); his attention gradually becomes

> **It is not the player who knows where the club should be who is successful; it is the player who knows where the club is.**
>
> DAVID FEHERTY,
> CBS sports commentator and former Ryder Cup golfer

riveted on the ball. Instead of trying to remember how to hit it correctly, he clarifies his goal and then pays attention to some detail of what he's actually seeing. This frees his subconscious to do what it's designed to do—to respond in the moment with what he already knows and/or to learn from what is actually happening. By changing what he's paying attention to, Jim is able to actually exceed his desired 66 percent improvement—in only ten minutes. His Focus increases his Faith (his belief in what he can do) and his Fire (his energy about doing it). By regularly giving this kind of discipline to his attention, Jim can learn far more quickly and, over time, become more consistent in executing what he already knows.

The Impact of Focused Attention

It was the principle of focused attention that enabled me to survive that day as I stood on l'Aiguille du Midi paralyzed by fear. I realized that unless I found something to Focus on that didn't threaten me, I was going to be in deep trouble. So I decided to Focus on the footprints of the person in front of me and not take my eyes off those footprints until somebody said, "We're there!" That was something I had Faith (or belief) that I could do. As I began to concentrate on the footprints ahead, my awareness of the drop on either side of me and the frightening stories I was telling myself about all the terrible things that were going to happen to me slowly began to diminish. Focused step by focused step, I put one foot in front of the other. As I did so, my Fire (or energy) began to increase, and I finally made it down that ridge.

Now whenever I'm in a situation where I begin to feel fear, my experience that day on the ridge returns vividly to my mind. It's helped me rewrite the story I used to tell about myself—that I couldn't perform if I felt afraid. It's released more of my Faith and Fire in every dimension of my life. It showed me that I *can* do things despite the fear *if I change what I pay attention to and how I pay attention.*

Focused attention can improve performance in any arena of life. One acquaintance of mine who is an extremely talented violinist decided to return to performing and instructing after several years of conducting orchestras. He was having a difficult time because his conducting had left little time for personal practice. When he tried to perform, he found himself feeling nervous and actually shaking. Together we sat down and reviewed a tape that had been made of a recent concert in which he performed a Paganini concerto. As we watched, we identified one point at which he simply closed his eyes and went into a different zone. It was the point at which he was focused completely on the music, and it was obvious that the interference was no longer there. As a result of recognizing what happened in that moment, he began to use the principle of focused attention to help himself improve. First, he focused on the shaking itself. He came to realize that the reason it was happening was because he was not breathing correctly from the diaphragm, and he was able to change how he breathed. Then he focused on his goal. Did he really want to perform? As he thought about it, he realized that despite his current discomfort, this was what he had been training for all his life. So he focused on doing things that would help him learn to enjoy performing. He lined up more performances. He practiced performing. He focused more on the music when he performed. As he did these things, he was able to regain his confidence and the joy he used to feel in making music.

Because of its impact in his own life, this violinist now uses the principle of Focus in working with his students. He recently told me, "When you get to the highest levels of violin playing, most players can play anything. So then it comes down to how you train the mind, how you can focus so that you can do the right thing at the right time with the right kind of confidence and your true talent can actually come out."

As well as with individual performance, the principle of focused attention delivers results in all kinds of team and organizational performance. In business organizations for example, focusing on a few critical variables of performance shifts attention away from interference such as politicking, complaining, backbiting and turf wars. In doing so, it unleashes Faith and Fire, facilitates the use of Knowledge, and transforms the organization into a truly "learning organization." In marriages and families, focusing on the critical variables involved in the accomplishment of a few shared objectives shifts the attention away from the arguing and positioning and one-upmanship that create interference. As a result, Faith is unleashed, Fire is ignited, and the performance results generate even greater Faith and Fire in family unity and achievement.

It really doesn't matter whether we're dealing with organizations, music, sports, academics, or the situation at home. The principle remains the same. In working to improve our own performance or helping others improve theirs, **potential is always blocked by interference. And interference is** *reduced—or eliminated—by Focus.* The challenge, then, is to manage our interference by finding a dependable, systematized way to create Focus.

Reflective Questions

- Think of a time when you performed or did something really well. Compare it to a time when you performed or did something badly. In each situation:
  — What "self-talk" or "story" were you paying attention to?
  — What beliefs did that self-talk/story represent?
  — How did that self-talk/story affect your energy?

- What fears do you have that might be creating interference? To what extent do you think these fears may be getting in the way of your performance? What specific effects do these fears have on your performance?

- Look at the Csikszentmihalyi model on page 41 and think of times when you felt
  — bored;
  — overwhelmed; or
  — confident and equal to the task.
  What do you think you could do to balance out your challenges? How might this affect your performance?

- In the coaching dialogue in this chapter, Jim improved his tennis swing by focusing on what the ball was doing. What are some things you might focus on to improve your performance

  — on the job, in making a presentation?

  — as a parent, in having a conversation with your child?

  — as a student, in taking an exam?

  — in some other area of your life?

Chapter 3: For an exercise that will help you

IDENTIFY AND FOCUS
ON CRITICAL VARIABLES

Access the online community at
Alan-Fine.com

Part 2

PROCESS

Creating Focus Through "GROW"

An expert is someone who has succeeded in making decisions and judgments simpler through knowing what to pay attention to and what to ignore.

EDWARD DE BONO,
British psychologist, physician, author, and consultant

There are a finite number of notes that the human ear can hear. And those same notes are available to us all. But there's a huge difference between the average five-year-old banging random notes on the piano and a concert pianist performing a classical concerto. There are no secret notes that the concert pianist has that the five-year-old doesn't have. The secret isn't in what the notes are. The secret is in the order and the manner in which the notes are played. If you don't have an effective process to help you learn how to play those notes in the proper order and with excellence, you may have all the tools to play great music, but you will never play it.

The same principle applies to the process of creating Focus. You may have all the tools you need (and you do), but if you don't have a simple, repeatable process to create Focus on a regular basis, you'll never create it. Your performance will consistently be impaired by interference and diminished Faith, Fire, and Focus.

In this chapter, we're going to explore a process that can enable you to create Focus in the one performance that affects every other—decision making. This is vital because whether you're trying to improve the way you play a Mozart concerto, increase your managerial skills, boost your organization's profitability, build a sales force, increase your fitness, refine your golf swing, or become a better parent, your improvement is a function of the decisions you make concerning how you're going to go about it. Another way to say it is this:

Every performance (or result) is a consequence of taking action, and every action is the result of a decision.

In other words, *decisions* lead to *actions* which lead to *results*.

Decisions → Actions → Results

Therefore, the more quickly and accurately we can make decisions, the more effectively we can create desired results.

Fast/Accurate Decisions → Effective Actions → Improved Results

I like to refer to the dynamics of the relationship between decisions, actions and results in terms of what I call Decision Velocity™. In sports such as tennis and golf, the term *swing velocity* describes the speed and direction[1] of the racket or club, which in turn controls the speed and direction (and therefore accuracy) of the ball. Obviously, the faster and more accurately you hit the ball, the more likely you are to win. This same combination of speed and accuracy has a similar effect on decision making and, therefore, on the results we get in any area of performance. Decision Velocity, then—or the speed and accuracy with which we make decisions—is critical to top performance in any area of life.

Both speed and accuracy are important to results. When we make fast decisions that aren't accurate, all we have is more mistakes. When we make accurate decisions that aren't fast enough, we lose valuable time and opportunity, and in many situations the competition gets ahead of us. Clearly, the more accurately *and* quickly we can make decisions, the more quickly and effectively we can improve. So the question is, How can we create the Focus that increases Decision Velocity and leads to breakthrough results? We can do it through a process called GROW.

GROW

Twenty years ago, I had the privilege of working with Graham Alexander and Sir John Whitmore—two of my former *Inner Game* partners—to develop a process that is now used by executive coaches and organizational-design experts worldwide. This process is called GROW. Basically, it is a map of human decision making. It provides a simple way to create Focus, reduce interference, and improve performance in any area of life. Having since recognized the vital roles of Faith, Fire, and Knowledge as well as Focus in top performance, I now place that performance model at the very center of the GROW process.

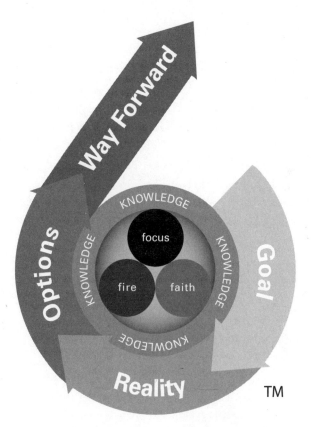

This is how GROW works. Whenever we make a decision, we eventually go through four phases. We think about the following:

Goal: What we want to do
Reality: The circumstances we're dealing with (or how we perceive them)
Options: How we might move from our Reality to our Goal
Way Forward: What action we want to take

But typically, we don't approach these elements sequentially. We may start in Reality. ("Oh, I am so bad at taking care of myself! I eat junk food. I don't exercise.") Then move to Goal. ("I really want to change my habits so I can feel better.") Then shift to Options. ("Maybe I should get some exercise equipment.") Then go back to Reality. ("No, I don't have a place to put it, and besides, it's really expensive.") Then back to Options. ("I know—I'll get a membership at the gym. John did that a few months ago, and he's looking great!") Then back to Reality. ("But that gym makes you sign up for a year. I have no confidence that I can do that for a year, and if I don't, that would be a huge waste of money. Besides, when would I go? I'm buried alive at work and hardly have time for my family as it is.") Then back to Goal. ("Maybe I should just set a goal to eat better.") Then back to Reality. ("But that is *so hard!* I've got a sweet tooth that won't quit, and it's hard to get healthy food when I have to travel. Oh, I just don't know what to do!") Finally, we move to (a very ineffective) Way Forward. ("I guess I'll think about it again tomorrow.")

Our thinking goes all over the place. It's like trying to score runs in baseball by running all over the field between stepping on the bases. It's not impossible; it's just a whole lot more difficult. And that difficulty significantly dampens our Faith and our Fire.

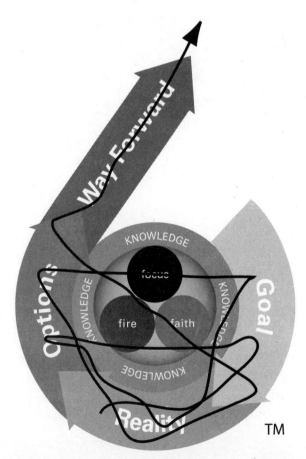

TM

However, by giving order, discipline, and Focus to these phases we go through, we can significantly reduce interference, increase the speed and accuracy of our decisions, and improve performance.

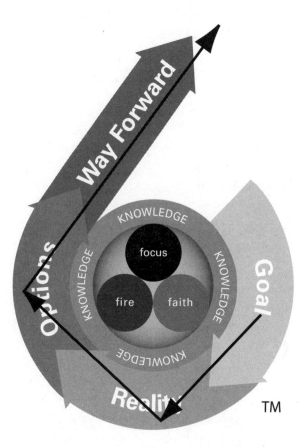

In harmony with the principles of Csikszentmihalyi's flow paradigm (see pages 40–42), GROW enables us to chunk down the challenge into doable tasks by creating a sequential Focus on each of the four phases. First we focus on our *Goal*—"What is it I want to accomplish or achieve?" Then we shift our focus to *Reality*. We clarify what's been happening, what we've tried so far, and the results we've been getting. We identify the obstacles we're facing, and then we reassess to make sure our Goal is still realistic. Then we focus on *Options*. We "brainstorm" to generate a wide range of ideas that could help us reach our Goal. At this point, we don't evaluate or judge; we just get ideas out—no matter how bizarre. Then we draw back and evaluate. We determine which options are viable and which tap into our Faith (we believe we can do them) and our Fire (we're excited about doing them). Finally, we focus on our *Way Forward.* We determine what we believe to be the best option(s) to move forward in achieving our Goal. By creating a way to Focus effectively, GROW releases Faith, Fire, and Knowledge.

Overcoming a Fear of Public Speaking

Let me share a personal example of how GROW works. I never liked public speaking. Maybe it's because as a child, I was painfully shy. Maybe it came as a result of having to face that scruffy six-foot jock on the tennis court when I was eleven. Maybe it came from my experience at twenty-one when I tried to coach a group of ladies in tennis and got so tongue-tied I couldn't get a word out. (At that point, the gorillas in my head were screaming so loudly I finally had to send the ladies away to hit some balls while I tried to regroup.) Whatever the reason, being in front of a group used to terrify me.

However, I knew that to be the coach I wanted to be, I would have to speak to groups.

So I focused on my Goal. What I wanted was to be able to speak without being terrorized. Next I focused on Reality. InterFEARence was getting in the way. A voice in my head kept saying, "They're judging you. They think you sound foolish. They're not listening to you. They're laughing at you." I would get physically tense. My mind would race, trying to figure out how to change the situation. The words coming out of my mouth seemed nonsensical. So I focused on my Options. I brainstormed and considered everything from delivering prerecorded speeches to imagining everyone in the audience in their underwear (as some speaking consultants suggest) to simply giving up and changing professions.

Finally, I decided on a Way Forward that involved focusing on two things. One was my posture. I knew that when I spoke well, I stood up straight and had a confident posture. When my posture was poor, I could sense the audience growing restless. I could see them looking at each other and rolling their eyes, and then I grew more afraid because I believed things weren't going well. It was a vicious cycle, and I wanted to interrupt the loop. I knew that my posture was something that I could control, no matter what. So I decided to make sure that I maintained good posture so that I would always look confident and competent in front of a group. (Top athletes have also used this focus on posture to improve performance.)

My other focus was on one or two "smilers" sitting close to the front of the room. In every group, it seemed there were always a few people who just naturally projected a kind of warm, fuzzy, positive feeling. When they would smile and nod, it made me feel good. It relaxed me. So I decided to start each presentation by talking to them as if they were the only people in the audience. Then once I got going and felt more comfortable, I would gradually expand to others and then eventually to everyone—even the "holdouts," who, by that time, I would be ready to take on one by one and bring on board.

So basically, I changed what I paid attention to. Instead of focusing on speaking to a large group of people (which seemed like a huge, scary thing to me), I focused on standing up straight and simply talking with one or two smilers. Those were things I knew I could do. Focusing on what I could control changed my Faith, which, in turn, increased my Fire and helped me dramatically improve my performance.

Over the years, I've used GROW to deal with everything from performance improvement in business and sports to improvement as a parent and as a personal coach . . . from dealing with economic challenges, when I didn't know where the next penny was coming from, to dealing with painful, judgmental thoughts when my first marriage broke up. ("Why did this happen?" "This is not fair!" "Why did she do this?" "What are people going to say?" "I'm going to be lonely." "Will I ever find anybody else?") I even used it to help me get through the pain during a flight home when I had a ruptured appendix. "What's my Goal? What's the Reality? What are my Options? What's the best Way Forward?"

GROW increases Decision Velocity. It helps reduce interference, clarify thinking, identify options, and chunk down the challenge into doable tasks. It unblocks Faith, Fire, and Focus and frees people to use the Knowledge they already have.

Other Applications of GROW

GROW can be used to improve decision making in any area of life—from determining corporate strategy to figuring out how to be a better parent or how to plan your day. It isn't rocket science. It's not some revolutionary new

Some Other Applications of GROW

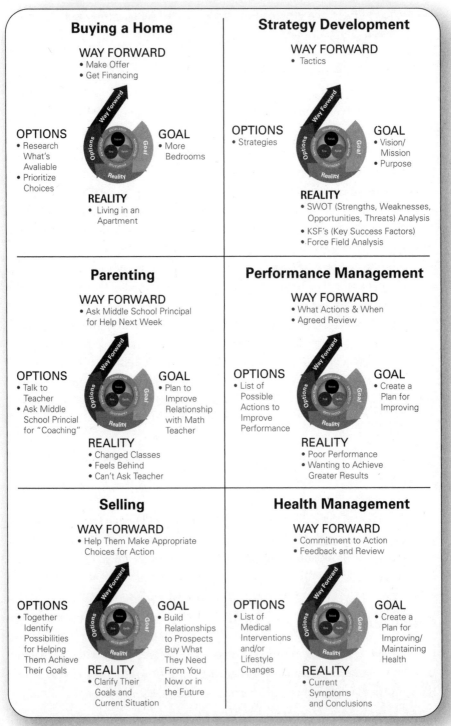

Buying a Home

WAY FORWARD
- Make Offer
- Get Financing

OPTIONS
- Research What's Available
- Prioritize Choices

GOAL
- More Bedrooms

REALITY
- Living in an Apartment

Strategy Development

WAY FORWARD
- Tactics

OPTIONS
- Strategies

GOAL
- Vision/Mission
- Purpose

REALITY
- SWOT (Strengths, Weaknesses, Opportunities, Threats) Analysis
- KSF's (Key Success Factors)
- Force Field Analysis

Parenting

WAY FORWARD
- Ask Middle School Principal for Help Next Week

OPTIONS
- Talk to Teacher
- Ask Middle School Princial for "Coaching"

GOAL
- Plan to Improve Relationship with Math Teacher

REALITY
- Changed Classes
- Feels Behind
- Can't Ask Teacher

Performance Management

WAY FORWARD
- What Actions & When
- Agreed Review

OPTIONS
- List of Possible Actions to Improve Performance

GOAL
- Create a Plan for Improving

REALITY
- Poor Performance
- Wanting to Achieve Greater Results

Selling

WAY FORWARD
- Help Them Make Appropriate Choices for Action

OPTIONS
- Together Identify Possibilities for Helping Them Achieve Their Goals

GOAL
- Build Relationships to Prospects Buy What They Need From You Now or in the Future

REALITY
- Clarify Their Goals and Current Situation

Health Management

WAY FORWARD
- Commitment to Action
- Feedback and Review

OPTIONS
- List of Medical Interventions and/or Lifestyle Changes

GOAL
- Create a Plan for Improving/Maintaining Health

REALITY
- Current Symptoms and Conclusions

approach or Nobel Prize–winning discovery. People have been trying to set Goals, deal with Realities, come up with Options, and decide on Ways Forward forever. GROW simply gives order, system, and language to the things we already do. The very fact that we all already do them is what makes the process so practical and simple. Even when the problem truly is a Knowledge (or "+K") problem, GROW provides a doable process to create Focus, reduce interference, and gain and then implement that Knowledge more effectively.

A few years ago I met with a regional sales manager who used GROW on the job at a small training company. In his second year, his revenue Goal was increased from $700,000 to $800,000. The Reality was that this was a tough goal. The economy was tight. A major client had decided to drop all classroom training. With the budgeting process, it typically took six to twenty-four months to realize any real revenue from new clients. So this manager was beating himself over the head trying to figure out where he could possibly get all this new revenue.

As he began to brainstorm Options with his boss, he gained a breakthrough insight. For years his mind-set had been that he would work with a client for a while until everyone was trained, and then that client would be ready to move on to something else. But suddenly he began to see the potential of focusing on developing more business with existing clients. His options list included such items as the following:

- Asking channel partners to introduce him to their client bases
- Asking for client referrals, including internal colleagues
- Recommending pilot sessions
- Utilizing his facilitator network to build awareness and expand interest
- Doing facilitator enhancement sessions or webinars

His Way Forward involved turning his options into a resource list he could draw on in working with each client and focusing on the few key clients that could produce the most revenue. He was excited about the possibilities and went to work. But then he hit a snag. He kept getting sidetracked. He finally realized his systems were getting in the way, so he decided to use GROW again with the Goal of coming up with a system that would work. The Reality, he determined, was that he was a highly visual person, and his current systems (planner, spreadsheet, client management software) were actually getting in the way. In brainstorming Options, it occurred to him that it might be helpful to add a large whiteboard on the wall so that he could keep the big picture constantly in front of him. That's what he pursued as his Way Forward, and it turned out to be another huge breakthrough for him. At any time—working at his desk, talking on the phone, or just thinking—he was able to look up at that whiteboard and immediately be reminded of his Focus. This manager told me:

> The net result of all my "GROWing" was that I not only met my $800,000 goal; I exceeded it by more than $11,000! And even in this difficult economy when one of my major clients cut programs, we were the one program they didn't cut. In fact, they almost doubled their training budget with us! Interestingly, this was a client whose business had been starting to dwindle before I made the decision to focus on current key customers. I am confident their business would have just petered out without the increased attention.

Using the GROW Questions

As I've worked with GROW in a wide variety of situations over the years, I've discovered that a few fundamental questions in each of the four areas make a significant difference in helping people clarify their thinking. These questions are listed below.

GOAL
What issue do I want to work through?

What do I want from this GROW "session" (meaning time devoted to resolving the issue)?

What are the consequences if I do not take action?

REALITY
Briefly, what's been happening?

What have I tried so far? What were the results?

What's my sense of the obstacles for me? For others (if others are involved)?

In what different way might others describe this situation?

Is my goal still realistic?

OPTIONS
Describe fantasyland. If I could do anything to make progress on this issue, what might I do?

If others are involved, what would they need to see or hear to get their attention?

If I were watching myself work through this issue, what would I recommend?

Do any of these options interest me enough to explore further?

If I were to act on this/these chosen option(s), how might I go about it?

WAY FORWARD

Do any of these options interest me enough to take action?

How will I go about it?

What might get in my way?

How might I overcome that?

What and when is my next step?

Eric*, a new manager, shared his experience with me in using these questions to resolve a difficult issue in his training company. (You can see his detailed notes as he went through these questions in Appendix A on pages 207–211.) When Eric had come on board, one of his major objectives was to expand company sales. He was excited to have inherited Scott, a high-performing business developer who had been able to fill the company's preview programs with thirty to sixty people while others hired to do the same job had been netting only ten to fifteen. But the compensation system was incenting Scott to create more leads than the sales reps could follow up on, and based on his performance, the company was paying him three times the industry standard for someone in his role. Theoretically, the system made it possible for Scott to actually earn more than the company was charging for the programs. In addition, as the company was increasing their number of programs, there was some concern that they were beginning to max Scott out.

Eric's Goal was to figure out how to provide enough leads for their regional sales people in a way that was affordable, didn't waste leads, and didn't overload a phenomenal business developer. As he went through the GROW questions in the Goal section, he realized that not taking action was not an option; he had to get this problem resolved.

In the Reality section, he noted that the preview programs had been the

---

* Names used in this and other personal stories throughout the book have been changed to respect the privacy of those involved.

primary source of new leads for the company and Scott had been doing 90 percent of the work in setting up those programs. (In other words, if Scott were to get hit by a bus or get burned out, the company would be in deep trouble.) He also noted the economic challenges of growing a business, problems with the compensation system, and the fact that Scott chose to do a lot of things manually, which made his approach hard to replicate. Faced with these Realities, Eric was surprised that when he brainstormed, he actually came up with quite a few Options. He could do the following:

- Create other lead generation pipelines besides the preview programs.
- Tell Scott he could do only a certain number of preview programs; if he wanted to earn more, he could move on to the position of client manager.
- Talk to Scott and find out why he was so good.
- Talk to Scott's peers and find out why they were struggling in the role.
- Help Scott increase his capacity by delegating some of the manual things he'd been doing, such as list building and administrative work.
- Change the compensation system to spread Scott's performance more evenly over all the regions.
- Reach out to some of his colleagues outside the company who were running their own firms, find out what they were doing with people in the same role, and see what they would suggest.

In the end, the Way Forward he decided on was twofold. His immediate action would be to benchmark with colleagues outside the company, explore the possibilities of changing Scott's compensation, and explore ways (automation or administrative help) that might help Scott leverage his efforts. In the near future, he would continue to develop a more robust marketing strategy and hire a marketing director to manage additional lead-generation activities, including trade shows, webinars, mailers, and facilitator support. In following up on his Way Forward, Eric said:

> In benchmarking with my peers in other companies, I discovered that most of them had two or three people working to fill each preview program, but they were still getting only ten or fifteen participants per session. I realized that paying Scott even three times the normal salary would be less expensive than paying three average performers salaries, commissions and

benefits—especially since those three people still wouldn't be getting anywhere near Scott's results.

In talking with Scott, I learned that he really loved his job and didn't want to move on—but he did want to make good money. We came up with a win-win compensation plan that incented him to fill each program with a manageable number of people and then move on to the next program. Although he wasn't putting exceptionally high numbers into each program anymore, he ended up actually increasing his earning potential. To make it happen, Scott agreed to let go of some of the things he was doing manually. We hired administrative help that freed almost three hours of his time each day and also significantly increased the number of people on his calling lists.

At this point, Scott continues to do a phenomenal job—only now he's able to do it for all seven regions. He's putting between thirty and forty-five people (which is manageable) in each program, so every region is having well-attended sessions that feed the sales pipeline. Scott is happy about the money he's making, and the increase in sales coming from his lead-generation pipeline excites him. I guess the biggest remaining challenge is to keep Scott away from buses, black cats, and ladders while we're expanding our marketing strategy.

Avoiding the Most Common Mistakes

Whether the issue is complex—like Eric's—or more simple, such as what to include in a speech or how to plan your day, GROW provides an easy way to increase Decision Velocity and improve performance. Over the years, I've found that one simple action in each phase of GROW will help you avoid the most common mistakes.

1. GOAL: Make sure it's S.M.A.R.T.

Goals are most effective when they are S.M.A.R.T.—Specific, Meaningful, Actionable, Realistic, and Time-phased. Not every goal needs to meet all five criteria, but by measuring the goal against each, you can ensure that it meets the criteria that are relevant and helpful to you in dealing with your current issue. Too many "goals" never get off the ground because they're vague and ill defined.

"S.M.A.R.T."

The acronym "S.M.A.R.T." has many variations, including the following:

S—specific, significant, stretching

M—measurable, meaningful, motivational

A—agreed upon, attainable, achievable, acceptable, action-oriented

R—realistic, relevant, reasonable, rewarding, results-oriented

T—time-phased, timely, tangible, trackable[2]

Whatever terms are used, the purpose is to help people make their goals more useful.

Almost always, a S.M.A.R.T. goal involves coming up with a doable *plan* to solve the issue or take advantage of the opportunity. Sometimes people forget that the Goal is *what needs to be resolved in the next half hour* (or however long they have for their GROW session). As a result, they set goals that are almost the equivalent of eliminating world hunger instead of trying to determine the most effective first step they can take now. That's why one of the first questions on the list is, "What do I want from this GROW session?"

---

2. REALITY: Make sure it's accurate

When we're working through issues on our own, it's easy to get caught up in our own version of reality. ("My boss is arrogant and demanding, and all my problems are his fault! Besides that, the other team members don't even carry their share of the load.") We never even consider other possible points of view.

The truth is that none of us is objective enough to see the entire situation as it really is. We all look at things from our own point of view. But if we can take the time to recognize our subjectivity, question our assumptions, and make a concerted effort to expand our thinking to include other perspectives, we have a far better chance of coming up with viable Options and a Way Forward that will actually work.

In checking the accuracy of our perceptions, it's helpful to watch out for assumptions and generalizations, particularly if they include blaming, accusing, and reactive language. ("It's all his/her fault!" "There's nothing I can do

The Fraser Spiral

Take a look at the picture below. Do you see a spiral?

If so, you might want to look again. Take your finger and trace any line of the "spiral." You'll discover that what you're actually looking at is a series of concentric circles.

This spiral is an example of the challenge of seeing things accurately.

about it!") In most instances, it's also helpful to ask, "What am *I* doing that's helping to create or add to the problem?"

3. OPTIONS: Make sure to really brainstorm

The most critical rule of brainstorming is to "suspend judgment and/or evaluation until all ideas are out." When we judge or evaluate an idea prematurely, we short-circuit the brainstorming process. It moves us into the watch-out mode and destroys the energy and momentum needed for brainstorming. It shuts down creativity. However, when we suspend judgment, we create an environment conducive to synergy and "piggybacking" of ideas. Often a particular idea that won't work can give birth to other ideas that will. Brainstorming means pushing yourself to think outside the box. It means not judging any idea until all ideas have been expressed.

4. WAY FORWARD: Make sure it's also S.M.A.R.T.

If the Way Forward is vague or ill defined, you can't execute it effectively. So it's helpful to use the S.M.A.R.T. criteria again (Specific, Meaningful, Actionable, Realistic, and Time-phased) to make sure your Way Forward is doable. It's also critical to make sure what you've chosen to Focus on is something that engages your Faith (it's something you believe you can do) and increases your Fire (you're excited about doing it).

In going through the GROW process, many people find it valuable to engage the help of a personal coach such as a friend, associate, or family member. This is particularly helpful in verifying or clarifying your perception of Reality and in expanding your awareness of possible Options. In the next two chapters, we'll talk specifically about how you can "coach" others to help them improve their performance through the GROW process.

Reflective Questions

- In what ways might your ability to make fast, accurate decisions affect your performance both on and off the job?

- Where do you tend to get off track in your decision making?
  — Not clear enough on the Goal
  — Not clear enough about Reality
  — Don't brainstorm enough Options
  — Way Forward isn't S.M.A.R.T.

- Are there areas in your life where you avoid making decisions? What are they? Where are you getting stuck (Goal, Reality, Options, Way Forward)?

- Are there areas where your decisions are not accurate because you make them impulsively or too quickly? What are they? What stage(s) of GROW are you neglecting to appropriately explore?

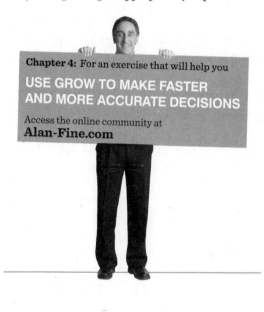

Chapter 4: For an exercise that will help you

USE GROW TO MAKE FASTER AND MORE ACCURATE DECISIONS

Access the online community at
Alan-Fine.com

Coaching for Breakthrough

One of the great challenges of coaching (or teaching or parenting) is to realize that the ultimate motivation for change has to come from the person being coached—not the coach.

MARSHALL GOLDSMITH,
author, professor, consultant, and executive coach[1]

I magine that you're ranked as the sixty-fifth best golfer in the world. Imagine what it would be like to have millions of people watching you as you compete against the world's #1 golfer in the first round of a professional match-play tournament. And imagine that in a previous interview, you'd made a comment about that person that was seen by many as derisive—"Anything can happen, especially where he's hitting the ball!" Now imagine that you lose to that person—in fact, not only do you lose, but you lose by the biggest margin possible. Can you even begin to envision the beating you would take from the press (as well as others) about your performance . . . and about your comment?

This is exactly what happened to professional golfer Stephen Ames when, in February of 2006, he made golfing history by losing "nine and eight" to Tiger Woods in the World Match Play Event in California (which is almost as badly as it's possible to lose).* As expected, the press raked Ames over the

---

* In most professional golf tournaments, the winner is the person with the least number of strokes after four rounds (or 72 holes) of golf. In match play, however, each of the eighteen holes in a round is a separate event, and the winner is the one who "wins" the most holes. "Nine and eight" means that one player has already won nine of ten holes played, one has been tied, and there are only eight holes remaining to be played. Obviously, there would be no way the player who was behind could possibly catch up.

coals, and in the post-match interview when Tiger was asked, "What's your message to Stephen Ames after his comments about you?" Tiger responded simply, "Nine and eight!"

Now fast-forward in your mind one month to the final round of the Tournament Players Championship (TPC)—golf's fifth "major" tournament—where Stephen Ames is pitted against forty-eight of the top fifty players, including Tiger Woods. This time, Stephen wins—by a remarkable six-stroke lead over his closest competitor and fifteen strokes ahead of Tiger Woods. As a result, he takes home the biggest check in golf history at the time ($1,440,000).

What made the difference? How could Stephen Ames recover from such an embarrassing loss and then go on just one month later to win by a huge margin on the very difficult TPC Sawgrass course in Ponte Vedra Beach, Florida—a course known for the wind, water hazards, and "fast" greens that were causing other players to fall apart all around him? He did it by using the very ideas we've been exploring in this book.

In this chapter, we're going to take a look at how we can use GROW to help others create breakthrough performance. In doing so, we'll use the word *coaching* to describe not only interactions such as those between an athletic coach and an athlete, a parent and a child, a manager and an employee, and a teacher and a student—but also any interaction in which one person is seeking to influence another (or others). And we'll use the word *performer* to describe the person (or persons) the coach is seeking to influence or help. Understanding this up front will help expand thinking beyond typical coaching situations as we talk about the power of the inside-out approach.

Less Is More

Prior to the Players Championship, I worked with golfer Stephen Ames to help him prepare for the tournament. Our Goal was to develop a strategy that would help him get into flow and maintain a high-performance mode on every hole.

At the time, Stephen's caddy was his brother, Robert. The Reality was that in trying to be a good caddy, Robert's Focus had been on giving Stephen yardages, advising him on club selection, and helping read the putts. He had been doing all the "correct" caddy things because he had Faith (or belief) that this was the best way to help his brother, and he had a lot of Fire (or passion) about doing his job right. The problem was that Robert's input—which was accurate and would have been useful to many players—was unintentionally creating interference for his brother. Stephen would overfocus on all the information Robert had given him, causing him to doubt his own instincts. As a result, he would begin to lose Faith in himself and Fire or commitment to what he was doing.

Stephen and I both knew that in order to play well, he needed to have a quiet mind. To achieve this, he needed to Focus on something he could control that would also increase the quality of his execution. We considered a variety of Options, but the Way Forward we finally chose involved enlisting Robert. We agreed that Stephen would tell Robert exactly what he planned to do with each shot. If Stephen failed to verbalize specifically what he intended to do on a particular shot, Robert would stop him and stand next to him until he did. We also agreed that Stephen (who is very kinesthetic) would use his hands each time to describe the shot, and that he would then tell Robert what he was going to Focus on as he was hitting the ball.

> I'm just going and try to stand over each golf shot and make sure that I'm clear and committed to what I'm going to try and do and stop worrying about the result beforehand . . . and hopefully everything will come out my way.[2]
>
> **STEPHEN AMES,** in an interview just prior to the final round of the 2006 Tournament Players Championship

Had you watched the media coverage of the event, you would have seen Stephen and Robert talking together often and Stephen using his hands as they discussed each shot. You would have heard the commentators say: "Stephen said this morning in the newspaper that what he wants from his brother is to help him paint a picture, and then let him—Stephen—make the decision." "You see [Stephen] working in concert there with his brother and caddy, Robert . . . a very good player in his own right . . . and he's very involved in his brother's game." "[Stephen's] having a great time with his brother, isn't he?" "Yeah, he is. And they're working well together as a team."[3] Both Stephen and Robert had a high capacity for performance, which included significant Knowledge about the game. As they each shifted their Focus, they were able to change their Faith—their belief in themselves and each other—which allowed them to be more Fired up about what they were doing together and to make use of the Knowledge they already had. This enabled them to take the actions that delivered breakthrough results.

In this case (as in most coaching situations), "less" truly was "more." As one of Stephen's coaches, I didn't tell him how to hold his club. I didn't tell him how to make his swing or hit the ball. What I did before the tournament—and what Robert did on the course—was to help Stephen Focus on his goal for each shot and then Focus on a specific aspect of one critical variable as he made the shot. This inside-out approach allowed Stephen to release his Faith, Fire, and Focus and do what he already knew how to do so well. It also empowered Robert to help coach his brother to a stunning win.

What Is Coaching?

The whole idea of helping others improve their performance is typically called "coaching." The idea is as old as the first human beings trying to help others along the way.

COACHING IN BUSINESS

In the business world, executive "coaching" became popular in the early eighties, but it was done on an outsourced basis and was seen essentially in a negative light—as a sort of remedial help for executives whose job performance wasn't up to par. During the nineties, the remedial view began to fade and business coaching became more popular. Associations were created to establish some kind of standardization. Certification from these organizations could take anywhere from three to eighteen months and cost thousands of dollars.

What's become more popular now is the idea of the manager or leader as a coach. In fact, today coaching is generally recognized as an integral part of a manager's or leader's job. In the words of one BlessingWhite report: "More than three-fourths (78%) of managers agree that coaching is a priority in their organizations right now. The reasons: the need to develop leaders, retain top talent, increase communication, and support the performance management process . . . [A] staggering 91% of managers told us they "like" or "love" to coach."[4]

Some suggest another growing trend is the creation of "coaching cultures" in organizations.[5] However, many organizations fall short because they still don't hold managers accountable for coaching or back up their expectations with clear initiatives and tangible incentives.[6]

Whether we're athletic coaches, business coaches, leaders, teachers, or parents, coaching can be a source of deep personal satisfaction. But it's important to keep in mind the reason *why* we coach. *We coach to generate results.* And if what we're doing doesn't have a significant, positive, measurable impact on results, then basically what we're doing is wasting everybody's time and money. Looking back, I realize now that, unintentionally, that's what was often happening when I was trying to teach the 10X girl and others to play tennis. I was being paid to get in the way of people's learning (or their children's learning), and we were all smiling about it because we all believed we were doing the best thing. But what we were doing was not producing breakthrough results. And unfortunately, many of us as coaches are still stuck in the story that *telling* people what to do will produce breakthrough results. In fact, even lack of Knowledge doesn't keep us from dispensing it—especially if we have a title (manager, leader, coach, parent), because in today's society, title implies expertise.

What goes under the banner of coaching today includes everything from counseling to consulting to mentoring to giving advice. Most of it comes from the traditional outside-in (+K) approach, and it tends to emphasize what the *coach* thinks the performer should do or pay attention to rather than what the performer actually can do or pay attention to. In terms of the GROW model, it represents the *coach's* view of what the Way Forward should be based on his/her assessment of the Reality. In chapter 1, I mentioned that there are times when this formula works. This happens specifically when four conditions are in place:

1. The coach knows the correct instruction to give the performer.
2. The coach can communicate instructions in a way that will capture the interest of the performer.
3. The performer is interested and wants to receive the coach's instructions.
4. The performer has enough awareness/experience to act on the coach's instructions.

The presence of all four conditions at once is rare. Why? Because of the following:

While coaches typically try to get performers to conform to what's worked for them or for others they've seen . . .	. . . "peak performers"—by definition—typically *don't* do things the same way as everyone else. Therefore, many coaches don't really know what instruction will actually be helpful to the performer.

While some coaches may be incredibly brilliant . . .	. . . many are unable to communicate in a way that actually speaks to the performer.
While some performers think they really want to learn . . .	. . . many are focused on imitating some popular role model or don't fully trust the intent or competency of the coach.
While some performers attempt to follow the coach's instructions . . .	. . . they have an awareness gap—a gap between what they think they do and what they actually do (see p. 12)—which keeps them from acting accurately on the coach's instruction.

Because these four conditions are not usually all present at once, *outside-in* coaching often creates interference rather than improvement. Let me give you an example. Some years ago, I was occasionally asked to talk about the psychology of golf at schools run by a golf magazine in England. My role there was simply to give lectures and did not include going out on the driving range with the participants. On the third day of one of these events, however, the magazine publisher took me aside in the middle of the afternoon and asked me to go down to the range to see if I could help an elderly couple who were taking up golf as their retirement activity. As I got close to this couple, I could see that the man was very frustrated and the woman was in tears. As I watched them trying to hit the ball, I could see that the man was making contact, but it was pretty erratic, and the woman was missing the ball altogether most of the time, though occasionally she would "top" it (just barely brush the top of the ball with her club).

I asked them what the golf pros had told them to do. It was simple, basic stuff—how to grip the club, how to stand, and how to turn. Those were certainly important basics to work on, but these people were definitely not having a good time. So I began to work with the woman. I said, "For just a few minutes, would you be willing to forget about all those things you've been trying so hard to do? Just swing at a few balls and tell me what you're noticing." She did, and within six shots, she started hitting the ball up in the air. It had a wicked hook on it, but she was thrilled because at least she was getting it up in the air. As this woman's mind had calmed down, her muscles had relaxed and she had gone back to what was comfortable—which was using a grip that closed the face of the club when she hit the ball. That's what was causing the hook. But now she was hitting the ball, and she was a happy customer. So now we could move on and talk about the possibility of incrementally trying to get a more effective grip.

This was a critical lesson for me about the importance of delivering the Knowledge component at the right time and in the right way. If it's delivered in a way that creates interference—that blocks a person's Faith, Fire, and Focus—it will not bring positive results.

The Inside-out Approach

The inside-out approach gives us a different way to think about coaching itself. It's far less about providing additional Knowledge than it is about releasing the Faith, Fire, and Focus that was inherent and natural in the performer as a child but is now suppressed by interference. It's not about looking at people in terms of what's wrong, broken, or missing; it's about looking at them in terms of what's inside that we can help get out. It's about removing interference and making it safe for people to dare to dream, to dare to think about what's possible—and then helping them find doable first steps.

Thus, a coach using the inside-out approach is always looking at an individual's performance through the lens of that person's Faith, Fire, and Focus as well as Knowledge. He/she is constantly asking, "Where is the person low—in the area of belief, passion, or attention? What is it that's getting in the way? How can I help remove it? What Focus will most significantly increase this person's Faith and Fire?"

Because belief drives behavior for the coach as well as the performer, a useful belief for coaches comes out of fifteenth-century Europe, when the word *coach* was used to describe a vehicle that conveyed valued people from where they were to where they wanted to go. In those days, "valued" people were probably those who had enough money to pay for the trip

> In every block of marble I see a statue as plain as though it stood before me, shaped and perfect in attitude and action. I have only to hew away the rough walls that imprison the lovely apparition to reveal it to the other eyes as mine see it.
>
> MICHELANGELO BUONARROTI, Italian Renaissance painter, sculptor, architect, poet, and engineer

from where they were (perhaps London) to where they wanted to go (maybe Manchester). In my experience, the most effective coaches are the ones who consider those they help as inherently valued people and treat them with dignity and respect even if they have to engage in tough conversations with them or even if there are things about them they don't like.

ORIGIN OF THE WORD *COACH*

"The coach was named after a small Hungarian village, Kocs, where superior wagons, carts and carriages were built . . . that would carry more than two people over the bumpy roads of the day in as much comfort as was then possible.

"One of the best of these multi-horse carts was called in Hungarian *kocsi szeker* 'a wagon from Kocs . . .' The German-speaking Viennese started to call this vehicle a *Kutsche*, which is how they heard Hungarians saying the name of the little carriage-making town. From Vienna these lively vehicles traveled to Paris and the French, adapting the Austrian word, called it a *coche*. In Rome it was, and still is, in Italian *cocchio*. Eventually the English borrowed the word and the vehicle and called it a *coach*.

"How then did a Hungarian horse-carriage word get applied to a basketball coach? Two theories have been offered . . .

"A coach was first a tutor who guided students through various fields of study or lessons. The coach carried the student through the course, as a coach and four might carry an 18th century English family to London. That is the commonly accepted theory.

"[T]he other British idea [is] that wealthy squires had their servants read to them as they drove in coaches about the countryside on their business or on long trips into a nearby city. A private tutor might come along to assist their children or indeed read aloud to the children, who would thus be "coached" in their studies as they proceeded along the country roads. It was only a short jump in meaning from an academic "coach" to one who coached in sports like basketball or football, who showed players, by virtue of his broader expertise and experience, some of the plays and tricks needed to excel in a particular sport."

Etymology used with permission of Bill Casselman, Canadian Word of the Day & Words of the World, www.billcasselman.com

Starting from "where they are" and taking them "where they want to go" is about getting into the performer's world. It's easy for coaches to get blindsided by what *they think* people have to pay attention to—to get so focused on the task that they miss the window through which a person can actually pay attention. What's helpful is for the coach to get into the world of the performer—to find the window through which the performer sees—and then ask him/her to look a little more carefully through that window. And if that window only allows someone to see one thing, to then work on that one thing and expand the view as the performer is able.

Think about the disaster movies in which the airline pilot has been injured and some passenger has to land the plane. The air traffic controller doesn't say, "Okay, you've got to level the aircraft via the altitude indicator, engage the triple-axis autopilot, descend at five hundred feet per minute as displayed on the vertical speed indicator, and lower the flaps to the approach configuration." Instead, he/she says, "Okay, what do you see?" The passenger might say, "I see this big, kind of wheel thing in front of me." Then radio control replies, "Okay. Take the wheel thing, slowly pull it out and turn it a tiny bit to the left." The person in radio control has to discover what's in the passenger's awareness and work through that; otherwise there's going to be a crash. Working through the performer's window is your biggest leverage as a coach. If you can understand even a bit of how a person processes the world, then you can enter that world and you can help.

THE PERFORMER'S WINDOW AT WORK

In *First Break All the Rules*, business consultants Marcus Buckingham and Curt Coffman drew from Gallup Organization interviews with more than a million employees over a twenty-five-year period to come up with twelve questions that "measure the core elements needed to attract, focus and keep the most talented employees." The questions are as follows:

1. Do I know what is expected of me at work?
2. Do I have the materials and equipment I need to do my work right?
3. At work, do I have the opportunity to do what I do best every day?
4. In the last seven days, have I received recognition or praise for doing good work?
5. Does my supervisor, or someone at work, seem to care about me as a person?
6. Is there someone at work who encourages my development?
7. At work, do my opinions seem to count?
8. Does the mission/purpose of my company make me feel my job is important?
9. Are my co-workers committed to doing quality work?
10. Do I have a best friend at work?
11. In the last six months, has someone at work talked to me about my progress?
12. This last year, have I had opportunities at work to learn and grow?[7]

By paying attention to questions such as these, astute managers and leaders can look through their performers' (or employees') window and better help them improve performance. As Buckingham and Coffman discovered, "those employees who responded more positively to the twelve questions also worked in business units with higher levels of productivity, profit, retention, and customer satisfaction."[8]

As we've observed, inside-out coaching is not as much *Knowledge* coaching as it is *Focus* coaching. Even when the issue involves Knowledge, it's about helping the performer *Focus* on the doable steps that enable him/her to gain or use Knowledge most effectively. It's not about solving the problem for someone; it's about helping that person solve the problem for him-/herself. It's about helping a person take full ownership for the solution.

Therefore, while a coach using the inside-out approach provides critical knowledge (such as the laws of physics, biomechanics, or competitive tactics in sports), his/her primary objective is to increase the performer's awareness by helping that person focus on and learn from real-time experience. And the more the coach can remove interference, the more quickly the performer will learn. This seemingly small shift in paradigm produces a big shift in behavior and results. Also, taking people "from where they are to where *they* want to go" is what releases commitment or Fire. While people may *comply* with what *we* want, they *commit* to what *they* want. And *commitment* makes all the difference.

> There is no contest between the company that buys the grudging compliance of its work force and the company that enjoys the enterprising participation of its employees.
>
> RICARDO SEMLER, author, CEO of Semco SA

The Responsibility (or Accountability) of the Coach

With my roots in sports coaching, I've become intrigued with the difference between how coaching accountability plays out in the sports world versus the business world. In sports, when an individual athlete or a team is not performing well, the coach gets fired. Why? Because the coach's job is to help raise the performance of the athlete. But in business, when the corporate athlete is not performing well, what happens? The "coach" (or boss) fires the corporate athlete! Why the difference? What is a corporate coach accountable for if it isn't the level of performance of his/her people? Why would we call someone a coach if he/she simply fires anyone who doesn't perform?

This brings up an interesting issue: What, really, is the role of the coach? And ultimately, who is accountable for performance—the coach or the performer? In the outside-in approach, accountability generally belongs to the coach. The coach is the expert. The coach knows what to do. The performer's role is essentially to listen and to execute the coach's instructions. But then the coach, rather than the performer, becomes responsible for the results.

In the inside-out approach, accountability is kept with the performer. He or she is responsible for the results. The coach's role is more of an "interference reducer." Why? Because, given the nature of human performance, the single most powerful thing the coach can do to improve it—particularly at the beginning—is to reduce the interference to a person's Faith, Fire, and Focus.

Until the coach reduces that, it's difficult for people to learn the Knowledge the coach wants to give them anyway. And if they already have the Knowledge, they can't perform effectively on that knowledge as long as they're struggling with interference.

Most of the difficult conversations we get into with people we supervise or are trying to help could be termed "accountability" conversations. They involve getting people to accept responsibility for performance—which is why they're difficult. Consciously or unconsciously, people often attempt to avoid that responsibility. Employees try to shift responsibility to their bosses. Students try to shift responsibility to their teachers. Children try to shift responsibility to their parents. After all, life seems easier when you don't have to accept responsibility for results.

WHO'S GOT THE MONKEY?

In "Management Time: Who's Got the Monkey?" (one of the two best-selling articles ever printed by the *Harvard Business Review*), William Oncken and Donald L. Wass give the highly visual and memorable description of shifting responsibility that has become classic in organizational thought. When a subordinate brings up a problem to his manager ("We've got a problem . . .") and the manager says, "Let me think about that and I'll get back to you," it's as if a monkey (responsibility) on the back of the subordinate suddenly leaps to the back of the manager. If the manager says the same thing to half a dozen subordinates during the course of a day, at the end of the day he has half a dozen rambunctious, screaming monkeys jumping around in his office—while his subordinates walk away with no monkeys at all![9]

With inside-out coaching, the accountability always remains with the performer. The role of the coach is to reduce interference and help the performer set S.M.A.R.T. Goals, explore Reality, identify Options, and create an effective Way Forward—a way in which the performer feels responsible to execute and for which he/she is accountable. Therefore, the coach is constantly

- looking at the gap between the Goal (what the person wants) and the Reality;
- looking for where in the three performance elements (Faith, Fire, or Focus) the obstacles show up;

- helping the performer decide what he/she needs to Focus on in order to get past those obstacles; and
- helping the performer find and commit to doable first steps.

In the end, coaching isn't all there is to being a manager or a leader or a parent. However, it's a powerful tool to use in any role when we're trying to help others improve performance. With that in mind, there are three critical questions you will want to always be asking yourself as a coach:

- Who is this about—the performer or me?
- When I speak, whose need is getting met—the performer's or mine?
- Am I reducing interference or increasing it?

Inside-out Coaching Conversations

So how do we go about coaching? The primary way we influence as coaches is through conversations with those we're trying to help. The approaches used to initiate such conversations depend on the performer's awareness of an issue and his/her willingness to engage in a conversation about the issue.

Look at matrix on page 81. Naturally, the most comfortable coaching conversations are those in the upper-right-hand quadrant, where the performer is both aware that a performance issue exists and is willing—even wanting—to address it. These kinds of conversations typically take place when someone takes action, such as signing up for tennis lessons, seeking help in upgrading professional skills, or asking for counsel or help. Such conversations are performer-driven; in other words, the performer owns the agenda and typically initiates the conversation. I call these "breakthrough" conversations because the purpose is to help the performer achieve breakthrough on his/her issue.

In contrast, conversations in the other three quadrants are coach-driven conversations; the coach has the agenda and initiates the dialogue. I call these "engagement" conversations. The purpose is to help the performer become more aware of a performance issue and willing to engage in addressing it. This is critical because you can't get to breakthrough until you have engagement. Therefore, engagement conversations are some of the highest return-on-investment conversations you will ever have. However, they are also some of the most difficult conversations you will ever have and, as a result, are often

Coaching Conversations

postponed or ignored. Having a scalable, replicable process to conduct these conversations effectively significantly increases the likelihood of creating engagement and therefore reaching breakthrough. It also significantly increases a person's comfort level in dealing with difficult conversations.

The distinction between breakthrough and engagement is critical from the very beginning. It clarifies who initially "owns" the issue and creates a significant difference in how a coach opens the conversation. In this chapter, we're focusing primarily on breakthrough conversations. We'll talk about engagement conversations in chapter 6. Keep in mind, however, that whenever we're in *any* conversation, we're in some stage of GROW.

Certain cues can help you quickly recognize whether you need to engage in a performer-driven or a coach-driven conversation. When someone asks for assistance ("Will you help me learn how to play tennis?" "Can you help me think this through?" "I'm stuck with something—can you help?"), that's a cue that you need to engage in a performer-driven conversation as described in this chapter. The performer is willing and aware. You'll want to use GROW to help the performer identify his/her own Goals, Reality, Options, and Way Forward. When *you* have the agenda—when you need to ask the performer to engage in resolving an issue because that person is unaware of the issue or unwilling to engage in a conversation about it—that's the cue that you will need to have a coach-driven conversation as described in the following chapter. You will need to own the issue until the performer buys in. Once the performer is engaged, you'll be able to move on to a performer-driven conversation.

Breakthrough Conversations

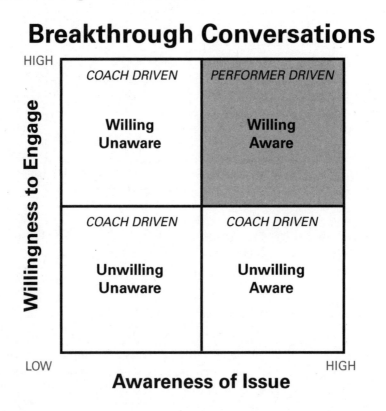

Breakthrough Conversations

	COACH DRIVEN	PERFORMER DRIVEN
	Willing Unaware	**Willing Aware**
	COACH DRIVEN	COACH DRIVEN
	Unwilling Unaware	**Unwilling Aware**

Willingness to Engage (HIGH / LOW)

Awareness of Issue (LOW / HIGH)

A good example of a breakthrough, or performer-driven, conversation is the discussion I had with Jim about improving his backhand (pages 42–44). I'm going to repeat that dialogue here—only this time, I'll point out the purpose behind some of the coaching questions.

Alan: So Jim, we've got ten minutes to work on your tennis. What would you like out of the ten minutes? [*I'm immediately getting into the performer's world by asking Jim to define the Goal. From the beginning, the agenda and accountability belong to him.*]

Jim: I'd like to be able to hit a backhand.

Alan: Now what do you mean by hit a backhand? [*To have a S.M.A.R.T. goal, Jim needs to be more specific, so I ask him to clarify. Note how the following questions encourage more and more specificity.*]

Jim: [*laughing*] In the court.

Alan: Like anywhere on the other side of the net? Is that what you mean?

Jim: No, I'd really like to hit it on this side of the court (indicating the opposite side across the net) in the lines.

Alan: Okay, so that side of the court, over the net, within those lines on the green. And how often would you have to do that?

Jim: Half the time.

Alan: Like five times out of ten?

Jim: Right.

Alan: Okay, how often do you think you can do it at the moment? [*We move into the Reality phase to ensure that we have a realistic Goal. Also, I'm getting data about his Faith—about what he believes.*]

Jim: Maybe two or three.

Alan: So, we're talking about a sixty-six percent improvement.

Jim: Yes.

Alan: Does that sound realistic to you? [*Notice there's no judgment here— just the question. This keeps accountability for success with Jim.*]

Jim: Sure.

Alan: Okay. So, if we could help you to knock five out of ten backhands into that half of the court, would that be worthwhile?

Jim: It'd be great.

Alan: Okay. What I'd like to do is throw you some balls, and let's see if you can really do three out of ten. [*We're still in Reality. We do this to test how accurate Jim's assessment of the situation is. I toss Jim ten balls. Two of them land where he wants them to go.*]

Alan: So what's your sense of how many you can do?

Jim: [*laughing*] Two or three. [*So Jim's assessment was accurate.*]

Alan: Okay. So is five out of ten still realistic? [*The responsibility for the Goal is still Jim's.*]

Jim: If you're a good coach! [**Jim tries to pass the responsibility for his success on to me.**]

Alan: [*laughing*] Okay. So, seriously . . . [**I gently shift the responsibility and accountability back to him.**]

Jim: Yeah, I'd love to do that.

Alan: When you were playing those shots, what did you notice? What got your attention? [**Note here that we continue to look at the situation through the performer's window, not the coach's. This distinction is key in maximizing performance improvement.**]

Jim: That I didn't have any confidence in my backhand. [**This is not the answer I expected.**]

Alan: How do you know that? How do you experience you're not confident? [**We're getting more specific on what Jim is noticing. I'm trying to turn his intangible feeling into something more concrete.**]

Jim: I'm just not watching the ball.

Alan: I'll throw you some more and just let me know what you are aware of that tells you you're not confident.

Jim: [*after hitting a few more balls*] Well, I'm *seeing* the ball. [**This is a big clue as to Jim's window on the world—what he's focusing on.**]

Alan: Okay. So, what are you *actually* seeing? Give me more detail about that. [**We're getting more and more specific.**]

Jim: [*continuing to hit more balls and commenting after each hit*] Well, I can see the line on it.

Alan: All right, tell me more about the line. [**Asking for more detail causes Jim to pay more attention.**]

Jim: The line was moving slow.

Alan: Okay. How about this one?

Jim: That was fast.

Alan: This one?

Jim: That was slower.

Alan: Okay. Now when you say they're fast, are they equally fast each time, or does it vary?

Jim: They vary a little, but it's hard to tell . . .

Alan: Could you put it on a scale where, say, "one" is slow and "five" is fast? [**Old habits die hard! I was inadvertently taking responsibility by suggesting the point range. It would have been better if I had asked Jim to come up with his own way to calibrate the spin.**]

Jim: Sure.

Jim: [*continuing to hit balls and comment*] That was a five. [*pause*] That was a seven.

Alan: Okay.

Jim: That was an eight. [*pause*] That was a ten! [**Not at any time in the conversation do I attempt to judge what Jim is doing as "good" or "bad," "right" or "wrong." Even when I ask him to judge the speed of his balls on a scale of one to five and he begins to respond with "seven," "eight," and "ten," I don't create more interference by pointing it out. By this time, most of the balls are landing where Jim wanted them to land.**]

Alan: All right. [*I stop throwing the balls*] Now just let me check something with you, Jim. What's your sense of how we're doing? [**The accountability and judgment are Jim's.**]

Jim: [*with a huge grin*] I'm doing a *lot* better. [**This is a clear indicator of increased Fire.**]

Alan: Do you know how many went in?

Jim: I think more than five.

Alan: Yeah, I think so, too. My sense is there are seven or eight out of ten going in.

Jim: That's great!

Alan: Is that what you wanted? [**I'm checking to make sure he has ownership of the results.**]

Jim: No—it's more! Thanks!

Jim actually improved his performance by even more than the desired sixty-six percent. And I gave him no technical instruction. (The two things I would have told him to do differently changed anyway). All I did was to help him pay attention in a way that enabled him to remove interference, tap into his Faith, Fire, and Focus, and therefore learn from his own experience.

In this situation, I happened to be a Knowledge expert. I knew exactly what Jim needed to do to improve his backhand. I could have told him: "Put your feet in this position." "Hold your racket like this." "Keep your eye on the ball." But then the accountability or responsibility for results would have been shifted to me because I was the one who was telling him what to do. In addition, Jim would have been distracted from his own learning experience with his body and the ball. He would have been thinking about what I was telling him instead of paying attention to what was actually happening. As a result, his Faith in his own ability would have lessened. His Fire would have dimmed because he would have been trying to comply rather than engage.

Also, Jim would have been dependent on me to tell him what to do next and to rate or judge his performance. We see this dynamic play out in a wide variety of situations, including in teams and organizations. When leaders simply tell people what to do (which is often the case), the result is often a lack of engagement and accountability on the part of the employee and little or no performance improvement. One of the primary observable signs of an outside-in approach is people constantly asking managers, leaders, teachers, or parents what to do.

With the inside-out approach, Jim became aware of, responsible for, and focused on his own experience. And the result in improved performance was dramatic. By simply changing Jim's Focus, we were able to change his performance, and changing his performance changed his belief. As a result, his Faith and Fire increased. In addition, he now had a way to improve his performance without my help.

THE NEUROSCIENCE OF LEADERSHIP

Research psychiatrist Dr. Jeffrey Schwartz and consultant David Rock have performed scientific research that demonstrates the measurable, physical effects of approaches such as inside-out coaching on Faith, Fire, and Focus. They observe that brain scan activity shows dramatic differences in the way people think. Because of these differences, giving advice or telling another person what your brain would do (which their research shows to be the most common way of trying to help people) is "very inefficient at facilitating change."[10]

They found that "for insights to be useful, they need to be generated from within, not given to individuals as conclusions."[11] When people experience their own moments of insight, it creates sudden bursts of high energy brain activity. It releases adrenaline-like and dopamine-like substances and creates new brain circuits that weren't there before. "Now because they create those circuits, they are energized by them, and they want to execute those circuits. They want to bring them alive in the world. So it's not, 'Communicate, communicate, communicate'; it's 'facilitate connections, facilitate connections, facilitate connections.'"[12] "The act of paying attention creates chemical and physical changes in the brain," say Schwartz and Rock. "Over time, paying enough attention to any specific brain connection keeps the relevant circuitry open and dynamically alive. These circuits can then eventually become not just chemical links but stable, physical changes in the brain's structure . . . The power is in the focus."[13]

Another Breakthrough Conversation: Ginny's New Job

In working on Jim's swing, we only used the first two dimensions of GROW (Goal and Reality) because execution was immediate. This is typical in the coaching of physical skills. But when execution is not immediate, Options and Way Forward become the planning steps that lead to future action. Let's now take a look at a breakthrough conversation that involves all four dimensions of GROW.

The following conversation was taken from a business coaching experience. The woman being coached—Ginny—was a former college administrator who had recently moved to a health-care company and was having some struggles. In this case, I was *not* a Knowledge expert. I'd never met Ginny before. I had no idea of what she was wrestling with, and I knew absolutely nothing about working in a health-care company. But I didn't need to know much about those things in order to help her. My objective was not to solve Ginny's problem for her but to help her solve it for herself. I didn't need to be a subject matter expert; I needed to be skilled at reducing interference and creating Focus.

The actual interview took only sixteen minutes. As you read the dialogue, you can see how the GROW process unfolds and the effect it has on Ginny's Faith, Fire, and Focus. Although you may not relate to the details of Ginny's job, the principles at work here apply across the board and can help you in almost any coaching or performance-improvement situation.

I've labeled each of the steps in the GROW process so that you can see how they naturally lead from one to the other and I've made a few coach's notes along the way. Particularly, I've marked a number of places where I've used "empathic listening" (sometimes referred to as "active" or "reflective" listening). This is a kind of listening in which the coach genuinely seeks to acknowledge and understand the performer's point of view—not necessarily to *agree* with it, but to *understand* it—and then to demonstrate that understanding to the performer's satisfaction by restating what the performer has said in his/her (the coach's) own words. Then the performer has the opportunity to either confirm or correct the coach's understanding. Empathic listening creates engagement. It allows the performer to examine his/her own thinking. It removes the interference created by the performer's driving need to be heard. Until that need is met, most performers can't really even take in what a coach has to say. Empathic listening is one important way a coach shows respect for a performer. Other ways include asking permission and being truthful.

THREE WAYS TO SHOW RESPECT IN COACHING CONVERSATIONS

Listen Empathically ("I value you enough to want to really understand your point of view—whether I agree with it or not.")
Ask Permission ("I respect your right to choose.")
Be Truthful ("I respect you enough to not lie to you or withhold from you, even if it makes you—and/or me—uncomfortable.")

Let's take a look now at my conversation with Ginny.

Goal

Alan: Ginny, we've got about fifteen minutes to have this discussion. So what would you like to get out of these next fifteen minutes? [*The question clearly establishes that the Goal is the performer's, and the time frame helps create Focus.*]

Ginny: I'd like a plan to be able to make some changes in the situation I'm in—a strategy or a way to do something about it or to handle it.

Alan: So if we could come up with something that would enable you to be in a position to take action, this would be a useful discussion. [*This is the first use of empathic listening. I restate what Ginny said to make sure I understand and also to make sure she feels understood. I'm also listening to make sure the Goal is S.M.A.R.T. (Future uses of empathic listening will be marked with an asterisk*.)*]

Ginny: That would be great.

Alan: Okay. Is it all right with you if I take notes as we do this? This is to keep me on track. And you can have them afterward if you want them. [*Asking permission and being up front about my reasons for taking notes shows respect, eliminates potential interference, and creates safety.*]

Ginny: Okay.

Reality

Alan: Okay. Briefly tell me about the situation. [*"Briefly" reminds us both of the time frame. There is rarely time to explore every detail, and I don't need all the detail to help her solve her problem.*]

Ginny: I'm in a new job. I've been there three months. After two months, I was promoted to team leader of a group. So not only do I have the position I was originally hired for, but I'm also responsible for this team.

Alan: Okay. So you've got one month in the newly promoted job, and two months prior to that. [*empathic listening*]

Ginny: Right.

Alan: And the new promotion means that you have responsibilities as a team leader. [*empathic listening*]

Ginny: Correct. It's fast paced. It's hectic. There's not enough time. I have some people who need a lot of attention, and others who don't engage at all. And my position is critical to the compensation, the reward structure, and everything for the rest of the team. And I can't seem to manage all of it.

Alan: So what I'm hearing is that you're struggling to do what you think is necessary for the team right now in addition to handling your own responsibilities. [*empathic listening*]

Ginny: Exactly.

Alan: Okay. Now what have you tried so far in order to resolve this? [*Her answer to this question will guide both of us in considering Options so that we don't try to "reinvent the wheel."*]

Ginny: I've gone from doing a whole lot and taking things over from the team to leaving them alone and saying, "Gee, you'll have to deal with it, and I'm sure you're good at it" to withdrawing from them to getting involved with them—I've sort of gone the whole spectrum, back and forth.

Alan: So you've done it for them, you've done nothing for them, and you've done everything in between. [*empathic listening*]

Ginny: Right. So they're having a bit of a tough time trying to figure out what my style is.

Alan: Okay. So there's confusion going on with them. [*empathic listening*]

Ginny: Oh yeah.

Alan: What else have you tried? [*"What else?" is a powerful question that can be repeated over and over to create greater levels of awareness. (Future uses in this dialogue are circled.)*]

Ginny: Just treading water. Just trying to get through each day, hoping that something will change on its own.

Alan: Okay. Anything else?

Ginny: No, that's pretty much it.

Alan: Okay. So has treading water and doing anything from nothing to everything for them made any difference?

Ginny: On a teeny basis, maybe, but I can see the long run is a problem. I'm just wallowing.

Alan: Okay. What do you suspect is in the way of resolving this for you?

Ginny: Not having enough time to do all the things I want to do. And possibly not identifying the things that need to be done versus what I think needs to be done.

Alan: Okay. So not enough time. Not clear on priorities. [*empathic listening*]

Ginny: Yes, and on my role with the others.

Alan: What else is in the way for you?

Ginny: The job itself is very demanding. It's very intense. Even if I plan what I'm going to do that day, whatever comes through the door is what we deal with, and sometimes that takes a couple of days.

Alan: Okay. So things that come up—or crises—get in the way of what you plan to do. [*empathic listening*] Anything else?

Ginny: I probably get in my own way. [**This is very insightful, very self-aware. It comes from a quiet mind that's not having to struggle with a lot of interference. And while Ginny might not hear this as feedback from someone else, she will pay attention to what comes out of her own mind and heart.**]

Alan: How?

Ginny: By stumbling along, trying to decide what to do, or not having a plan of action. I think that I'm actually eating up more time and energy than I need to.

Alan: Okay. Now what about for your team members? What do you suspect is in the way for them, keeping them from doing their best?

Ginny: Well, I'm probably in the way some. I've got a learning curve that I'm struggling with. And my inconsistent manner—at least that's how they perceive it at the moment—is probably in their way. [**Again, this is very insightful.**]

Alan: Anything else?

Ginny: I think that's basically it.

Alan: Okay. So obstacles that I'm hearing are not enough time, unclear priorities, the demanding nature of the job, and crises that keep coming up. And stumbling along at it is probably just prolonging the issue. [*empathic listening*]

Ginny: Yes.

Alan: And for the group, your inconsistency. [*empathic listening*]

Ginny: And probably the distribution of work. It could be that some of the work is sitting in the wrong places among the team members.

Alan: All right. So I'll put down "distribution of work." [*empathic listening*]

Options

Alan: Now, would you be willing to brainstorm with me for a few minutes?

Ginny: Sure.

Alan: Sometimes I call this "fantasyland." What that means is that, as we have this piece of our discussion, any idea—however crazy—is valid. So you can be as ridiculous as you like. You can be as realistic as you like. Let's just get every idea down that we can think of. [*I want to encourage Ginny to be totally free to brainstorm, to not worry about feeling judged or being in watch-out mode.*]

Ginny: So if the world were perfect, what would I do?

Alan: Yes. And the way you phrased that is important: If the world were perfect, what could *you* do? [*"If the world were perfect" (focusing "out there") could become an excuse for lack of action or success. By reaffirming "what could you do," we keep the Focus and the responsibility/accountability with her.*]

Ginny: Okay.

Alan: So what kinds of stuff might you do to resolve this in fantasyland?

Ginny: I'd have more time. I'd have more help.

Alan: Okay. [*As she comes up with options, I list them on my notes so that she can review them to help her choose her Way Forward.*]

Ginny: I might have different help. Maybe some of the team members would be different ones.

Alan: All right. More time. More help. Different help. [*empathic listening*] What else?

Ginny: I would probably be able to hook up my computer at home to take care of maintenance things so that I could be more available for decision making at work.

Alan: Okay. Computer at home. [*°empathic listening*]

Ginny: Also I would [*pause*]—we're in fantasyland, right?

Alan: Yeah.

Ginny: [*long pause*] In fantasyland, I would just let go and they would do all this stuff and we would have this just magic connection all the time.

Alan: Okay. So you'd let go and they'd do it. [*°Empathic listening—also notice there's no judgment here—no right/wrong/good/bad.*] What else?

Ginny: I would be more proficient at my piece of the whole pie. [*After a quick trip to fantasyland, Ginny is ready to move back to more realistic options.*]

Alan: Okay.

Ginny: And I would change the way we do some of our work. Redistribute it. Do almost anything to shake it up and start it again.

Alan: So just . . . start over. [*°empathic listening*]

Ginny: Yes.

Alan: Okay. Now what if you were in your team's shoes? What would you request of Ginny right now to help you? [*I'm encouraging Ginny to look at the issue from another perspective.*]

Ginny: I think I'd say, "Gee, what I'd like you to do is back off. Just let me go, but move obstacles out of my way when I run into those that are bigger than I am."

Alan: So one thing they'd want you to do is to back off and just remove obstacles. [*°empathic listening*]

Ginny: Some would. Others would say, "Sit right beside me. Make sure I'm doing okay. And tell me how well I'm doing along the way."

Alan: So others would want you to work closely with them and give them lots of praise. [*°empathic listening*]

Ginny: Yes.

Alan: All right. Anything else?

Ginny: Others would be happy to work in their own little cocoon and only once in a while come up and check in.

Alan: Okay. So leave them alone? [*°empathic listening*]

Ginny: Uh-huh.

Alan: Anything else?

Ginny: That's it in a nutshell from the team. I think that is what they would say.

Alan: Okay. Now if you could sit over here where I'm sitting and be Ginny's consultant, what advice would you give yourself? [*This encourages Ginny to consider yet another perspective.*]

Ginny: Oh, this is easy. I've got a list! Be patient. Just let some time go by. Lighten up on the team, meaning don't worry so much about everything I think I have to do. Some of it they really can do. They were there before me. They functioned without me, and they were a high-performing team to begin with. [*As her comment demonstrates, much of what I might have recommended as a coach (the "+K") she already knew. But how much of it would she have actually "heard" and been committed to implement—and how much would have created interference—if it had come from me instead of her?*]

Alan: So lighten up and trust them. [*empathic listening*] Okay, what else?

Ginny: Um . . . Learn your own job better.

Alan: ⟨Anything else?⟩

Ginny: Take a look at what I do in a day and move some of those maintenance items out of the office so that I can be more available to the team.

Alan: Okay. So, do the maintenance stuff at home. [*empathic listening*]

Ginny: Yes.

Alan: Okay. ⟨What else?⟩

Ginny: [*long pause*] I think that's mostly what I'd tell myself.

Alan: Okay. Now as I've listened to you, there have been a few thoughts that have come into my mind. Would you like me to share those with you? [*I'm asking her permission to share some ideas that have occurred to me—again acknowledging that the accountability is hers, not mine. It's more effective to share these ideas after she's gotten all of her own ideas out. This keeps me from wasting time suggesting things she already knows.*]

Ginny: Okay.

Alan: One of them is that you could go to the team and ask how they would like you to work with them. So I guess I'd say, "Ask for help." And the issue is, "How can I best support you in my new position?" [*As I wrote Ginny's options on the list earlier, I left several spaces in between in which I now write my own suggestions. This blurs the line between her ideas and mine.*]

Ginny: Okay.

Alan: Another thing you could do is use the very framework within which we're having this discussion with the team. In other words, you could create a kind of structured discussion around the issue that I think could be very productive.

Ginny: Okay.

Alan: So I'm going to add "Use this process" to the list. Also, you could delegate more to free you up to do the priorities.

Ginny: Okay.

Alan: In addition, you could also have team members "co-coach." That's where you teach them the skills of coaching and then have them support each other.

Ginny: So that it doesn't all funnel to me.

Alan: Yes. And you might consider that a version of delegation. So those were the things that were floating around in my mind. Now let me play back to you what we've discussed in fantasyland so far. [*empathic listening*]

Ginny: Okay.

Alan: [*showing her the list*] You could create more time, be patient and let more time go by, get more help, lighten up and trust team members more, get different help, learn your own job better, get the computer and do stuff at home, let go and assume people would just get on with it anyway, ask people for help, be more proficient at what you do, use this process we're going through now with your team, redistribute the work, delegate, start over, set up co-coaches, back off and just remove roadblocks, work closely with and praise some and leave others alone. That's the stuff we've been talking about. [*empathic listening*]

Ginny: Okay.

Alan: Now do any of these options interest you enough to explore further? [*Throughout this conversation, I've been observing Ginny's body language and watching for other evidences of her Faith and Fire—what she believes and what possible solutions excite her. But here's where we begin to get more verbally explicit.*]

BODY LANGUAGE

Empathic listening involves more than simply listening to words. It involves listening to things such as tone, inflection, emotion, and body language—the nonverbal cues that can communicate even more than words.

Body language makes up a larger part of communication than you might suspect. In their book, *The Definitive Book of Body Language,* CEO of Pease International Barbara Pease and author Allan Pease share that "Albert Mehrabian, a pioneer researcher of body language in the 1950's, found that the total impact of a message is about 7 percent verbal (words only) and 38 percent vocal (including tone of voice, inflection, and other sounds) and 55 percent nonverbal. . . . Anthropologist Ray Birdwhistell pioneered the original study of nonverbal communication—what he called 'kinesics.' . . . Like Mehrabian, he found that the verbal component of a face-to-face conversation is less than 35 percent and that over 65 percent of communication is done nonverbally."[14]

Ginny: I think so. Delegating and co-coaching.

Alan: Okay. Delegating and co-coaching. [*empathic listening*]

Ginny: Getting hooked up on the computer at home.

Alan: Any others?

Ginny: I think those would get me going. What I'm thinking on the delegating and co-coaching is that in a regular meeting, I could not only ask certain people to do certain things that I am currently doing, but I could also throw some things out on the table and let people choose some things they wish to be involved in.

Alan: So as I hear it, you're also rolling that in with "asking for help." [*empathic listening*]

Ginny: Yes.

Alan: All right, so those four—getting the computer at home, asking for help, delegating, and co-coaching. Those four are the options that interest you most? [*empathic listening*]

Ginny: Yes.

Alan: Now if you were going to do these, how would you go about it? [*I'm eliciting more detail to help her assess whether or not her ideas are realistic.*]

Ginny: Getting the computer at home is easy. That's contacting the Information Services Department and getting hooked up at home, and giving a good rationale as to why.

Alan: Okay.

Ginny: And the others would require looking at the assignments we have and figuring out which ones, in my opinion, could be done by someone else . . . and then presenting that to the team in a meeting.

Alan: Now, let me make sure I've understood this. You'd do some prework and then you'd present your thoughts to the team. And also at that meeting, you would ask for help. [*empathic listening*]

Ginny: Right.

Alan: And the co-coaching?

Ginny: I'd do that at the same time. I'd divvy out some of the jobs and ask for help, and then I'd use actual jobs or assignments to practice the co-coaching.

Alan: Okay. So I think I'm hearing two things here. First, you'd roll three ideas—delegating the work, co-coaching, and asking for team thinking—into a team meeting. And you're saying you'd have to do some prework to think about how you would deal with these issues and prepare your thoughts in advance. [*empathic listening*]

Ginny: Right.

Alan: And second, you'd contact Information Services to check out how you could get a computer hooked up at home. [*empathic listening*]

Ginny: Yes.

Way Forward

Alan: Now does doing those things interest you enough for you to take action? [*In other words, "Does it tap into your Fire?"*]

Ginny: Oh yeah. Definitely.

Alan: So if you were going to do them, what would be the first thing you would need to do on leaving this discussion?

Ginny: Take a look at the job list and do some prioritizing.

Alan: In other words, do the prework. [*empathic listening*]

Ginny: Right.

Alan: Now when would you do that? [*We're doing more here to ensure that her Way Forward is S.M.A.R.T.*]

Ginny: Tonight . . . because we meet first thing in the morning as a team. So I'd like to be able to present it to the team and talk with them about it first thing in the morning.

Alan: Okay. So you'd do the prework tonight and then present it to the team in the morning. [*empathic listening*]

Ginny: Right.

Alan: So if I were to call you last thing tonight or first thing in the morning, you'd be able to tell me . . . [*I watch her reaction carefully. If she hesitates, it tells me I haven't helped her break down the challenge of her action step to a level where she thinks she has the skill to meet it. I'm checking her Fire.*]

Ginny: What would be better is if you would call me tomorrow night because then I'd have an idea of how it went and what I'm going to do from there. [*Ginny's on Fire! She's taking so much responsibility that she says, "No, coach! I have a better idea."*]

Alan: Okay.

Ginny: Also, I could talk to Information Services during the day and get that taken care of so I'd know whether or not I can get hooked up at home. So by tomorrow night, I would have a lot more feedback on how it went, what I thought about it, and what I think my next step is.

Alan: Do you want me to call you? [*Now I'm appropriately asking permission.*]

Ginny: That would be great! I need a reminder.

Alan: Okay, so I've got an action out of this, which is to call you tomorrow night. Now let me check with you. What we've got to is some prework for you tonight and then the meeting with the team and the discussion with Information Services tomorrow. [°*empathic listening*] Now, does that give you what you wanted from this discussion—which, as I remember it, was a plan of action about how you were going to deal with this whole "too-much-to-do," "new-to-the-team" issue?

Ginny: I think I'm on my way.

Alan: Are you happy with where we've got to? [*I'm checking to make sure she got what she wanted out of the conversation.*]

Ginny: I am happy with it.

Alan: Okay. Do you want these notes?

Ginny: Yes. Thank you very much.

Alan: My pleasure.

Again, this conversation took only sixteen minutes. It helped Ginny change what she was paying attention to, which was interference created by the "big dilemma," including concerns about her own inexperience, too much to do, lack of role clarity, time management issues, and all the internal conversation that went with it—"How am I going to solve this?" "I'm getting in the way of team members." "This role is critical, and I'm going to let people down." By helping her shift her focus to the simple stages of GROW and the specific questions in each stage, we were able to break her world-hunger-size dilemma down to a challenge she believed she had the skill to manage. By changing her Focus, we changed what she believed was possible (her Faith), which increased her Fire.

GROW QUESTIONS TO USE IN COACHING

Below are some key questions that I use during a coaching dialogue. Obviously there are other questions that could also be useful. However, these questions have proven to work in a wide variety of circumstances. Particularly if you're new to inside-out coaching, I suggest you simply use these questions first in any situation. They will drive almost any issue forward in a constructive way.

Goal

What topic do you want to discuss?

What do you want from this discussion? (What's your S.M.A.R.T. goal?)

What are the consequences if you do not reach this goal?

Reality

Briefly, what's been happening?

What have you tried so far?

What were the results?

What's your sense of the obstacles for you? For others (if others are involved)?

Is the goal still realistic?

Options

Describe fantasyland—if you could do anything, what might you do?

If you were the other person/people, what would you have to hear/see to get your attention (assuming others are involved)?

If you were watching this conversation, what would you recommend?

Would you like suggestions from me?

Do any of these ideas interest you enough to explore further?

If you were to do this, how might you go about it?

Way Forward

Does this option interest you enough to take action?

How will you go about it?

What might get in the way?

How might you overcome that?

What and when is the next step?

The High-Performance Difference

Changing the Focus, thereby changing the Faith and Fire of performers, typically brings measurable—sometimes dramatic—performance results. The manager of one call center in a major U.S. corporation told me recently that out of eight teams at the center, his was the lowest performing. He said the situation was particularly difficult because his team of ten to fifteen specialists per supervisor was up against teams that had twenty-five to thirty specialists per supervisor. In addition, he had specialists coming to him saying, "Our supervisors seem to think they're always right. They're telling us what we have to do, but they're not explaining why, and we need to understand the 'whys.'" At the next staff meeting, this manager walked his supervisors through the GROW process and asked them what they thought. They decided they wanted to use it with their specialists, and the decision was made that they would report back in two weeks. This manager said:

> As I walked around the call center during the two weeks, I couldn't help but notice the change in the expressions on people's faces. Before, when the specialists would be asked to "sign off" (leave the phone to meet with their supervisor for individual coaching), they did it with the feeling that they were going to be told what they were doing wrong. But after a couple of sessions with GROW, the feeling was more like, "All right! My supervisor's going to ask me how it's going, and I'm going to get some good information here today!" I don't want to say it was an overnight change, but it really was one of those situations where you could see the improvement almost immediately as you walked around and just looked at people.

By the time this manager met with his supervisors two weeks later, he said the change in morale had been amazing. He had even had one specialist tell him she felt like she had a new supervisor. She said she didn't know what had happened, but now instead of being told what to do, she was being asked questions that allowed her to think things through and come to conclusions on her own. Others who had felt like what they were doing was just a job said they now felt they were on a career path. Some who had even been interviewing and sending out résumés for other jobs had stopped doing so. They said they were excited about their work and wanted to stay. Most exciting of all, he said, when the supervisors shared their numbers, they discovered that their group had moved from bottom-performing group to second place—in only two weeks!

A COMPARISON	
OUTSIDE-IN COACHING	**INSIDE-OUT COACHING**
Primarily giving advice (sharing Knowledge)	Primarily questioning, drawing out, removing interference
Judgments (good/bad, right/wrong, etc.)	No judgments (no good/bad, right/wrong, etc.)
Responsibility/accountability with coach	Responsibility/accountability with performer
Focus on what the coach believes should happen	Focus on what is actually happening
Generally less time spent in communication up front	Generally more time spent in communication up front
Coach required to be subject matter expert	Coach not required to be a subject matter expert
Tends to stifle creativity	Tends to encourage creativity

Another manager in a multinational corporation shared with me how GROW helped improve performance by empowering one of her reports to resolve issues on his own. She said that one day shortly after training her team in the use of GROW, she found the following voice message on her machine: "Lisa, I need your coaching on a situation. So you can prepare for our conversation, here's an overview. My Goal is . . . [*he explained*]. My Reality is . . . [*he explained*]. The Options I've thought of so far are . . . [*he shared them*]." Then there was a long pause. "Wait. Now that I think about it, I know what I need to do. Never mind; you don't need to call me back."

GROW gives Focus to the performer and Focus to the work of the coach. In doing so, it enables both to perform better and achieve better results.

In this chapter, we've talked about how to use GROW in "performer-driven" conversations. These conversations take place when the performer is aware of a performance issue and is willing to engage in a conversation about it. Coaching people in these circumstances is typically the easiest kind of coaching and is generally highly rewarding.

In the following chapter, we'll talk about how to use GROW in the more difficult engagement or coach-driven conversations when the performer is unaware that there's an issue, or especially when—aware or not—he/she is unwilling to engage in resolving it. In these situations, the challenge shifts from "taking valued people from where they are to where they want to go" to "taking valued people from where they are to where *we* want or need them to go." As I've said, these conversations are some of the highest return-on-investment conversations we will ever have. But they are also the conversations we tend to put off or avoid—unless we have a simple, effective process to make them happen.

Reflective Questions

- In attempting to coach or help others:
  — How often do you give advice?
  — How often is that advice acted upon?
  — How often is it carried out as you intended?

- When you give advice, typically:
  — Does it reduce or increase your performer's interference?
  — Whose need is being met—your performer's or your own?

- What has been the long-term effect of your coaching approach on your performer's Faith, Fire, and Focus? How do you know?

- Is there a situation in your work or personal life where inside-out coaching could make a positive difference in your ability to help others? How might you begin to utilize this approach?

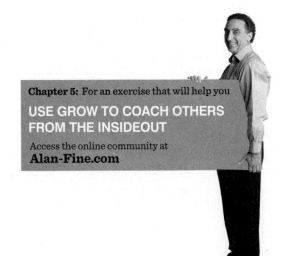

Chapter 5: For an exercise that will help you

USE GROW TO COACH OTHERS FROM THE INSIDEOUT

Access the online community at
Alan-Fine.com

Coaching for Engagement

Our research has shown that strong relationships, careers, organizations, and communities all draw from the same source of power—the ability to talk openly about high-stakes, emotional, controversial topics.

FROM *CRUCIAL CONVERSATIONS* BY KERRY
PATTERSON, JOSEPH GRENNY, RON MCMILLAN,
AND AL SWITZLER

Neil seemed to be going into a death spiral—not showing up at work, becoming more and more closed in his communication, and withdrawing from everyone. I was worried about his performance on the job, but even more, I was concerned about his personal well-being. Not only was Neil a business partner; he'd been one of my best friends since I'd moved to the United States. He shared my love for British humor—especially Monty Python. (What more can I say?)

I knew Neil was under a lot of stress. We'd made some changes in the company, which he'd clearly misunderstood and taken personally, feeling that his contributions were no longer valued. In addition, he was dealing with significant problems in his personal and family life. From my experience with Neil, I knew he wouldn't want to talk with me about these things; he would prefer to pull inside himself and try to deal with them on his own. However, his current behavior was clearly damaging his performance, his relationships—both personal and professional—and his health and peace of mind. And it wasn't solving anything; it was making things worse.

To be honest, I was reluctant to engage in a conversation with Neil. Based on past experience, I knew that he knew which buttons to push with me, and he was very good at it—better than most. I knew that confronting him would almost certainly be painful for both of us, and that created a lot of interference for me. I also struggled with a moral dilemma. I had concluded that it was legitimate for me—as owner of the company—to say, "Neil, we need to talk." But because of the other, deeply personal issues involved, I wondered— was it also legitimate for me to say "Neil, we need to talk" as a friend? I felt it was not my job to tell anyone which path he/she should be walking in life. But I felt less clear about my role in helping Neil see what his choices were and where those choices might lead. It made me think very carefully, and in the end I had to ask myself, "If this all comes off the rails and I didn't do anything, could I live with that? Would I be able to say, 'Alan, you gave it your best shot'"? At that point, the answer was "No." Once I realized that, it freed me to say, "Okay, so how far am I willing to go?"

I finally came to the conclusion that unless Neil determined to call in the police to haul me away, I would insist on having a conversation. And if he wasn't initially willing to talk with me, I would go to his house and camp out on his front porch until he was. That decision freed me to engage. At first Neil tried to stiff-arm me. He came up with all kinds of excuses why he couldn't talk with me. I told him his excuses were not going to work. He didn't have to talk with me right then, but if he hadn't set up a time to talk within three days, I was going to show up on his doorstep. As I'd anticipated, he tried to push my buttons. "You're not running this company right!" "You're overstepping your bounds!" "You have no right to interfere in my personal life!" I felt judged. I felt myself tensing up, wanting to defend, to justify, to fight back. But I knew that those kinds of responses would create interference, that they would get in the way of communicating and helping.

So I let Neil express whatever version of Reality he wanted to express, and most of the time I didn't react; I just listened empathically and said, "Yeah, I hear you." Sometimes I added, "But I see it differently." When he'd lash out at me, I'd say, "It's your right to say those things if you want. But whether you agree with me or not about the need to talk, I'm going to insist on it because I care. And that's my right. Look, if you prefer, this is not about you, it's about me. I truly believe it's in your best interest to talk with me, but even if you don't believe it, I've got to do this for my sake because I can't live with myself if I don't."

Finally, Neil began to realize that I really did care and that I was not going anywhere. He could scream, shout, rant, rave, or try to disappear, but none of that was going to make any difference. The only way he could get rid of me was to call the police; short of that, I was going to be there for him and we were going to talk.

In the end we did talk. In fact, we had a remarkable conversation. I had used the GROW process on myself ahead of time to prepare so that I could be clear on my objective, reduce as much of my own interference as possible, and come up with ways to help Neil reduce the interference that was getting in his way. I did a lot of empathic listening. I sincerely tried to understand where he was coming from and to let him know I understood—even though I didn't necessarily agree. I did a lot of affirming, both of him and of his role in the company.

Finally, Neil felt safe enough to let go of his fear of being judged. He was able to shift his Focus away from all the blaming, accusing, and defending and to get in touch with what he was actually thinking and experiencing. He could say, "Yeah, these are the choices I've made and this is the result. What have I been thinking? Maybe there is another way to look at all this that would lead to better choices and better results." As Neil focused on what was actually happening, I could see his interference start to clear and his Faith and Fire begin to grow. He was able to look at other Options and come up with a Way Forward that inspired confidence and hope.

While I knew our conversation had been cleansing and healing for Neil, I was truly amazed a couple of days later when I asked him to come into the office for a meeting. In a 180-degree turn from his recent behavior, he replied easily, "Sure, I'll be there." I was even more amazed when he began to share his experience with everyone at the meeting, and to do it with a profound sense of self-awareness and discovery. It felt as though Neil was in a completely different—and better—place.

Even with the Knowledge and experience I have in coaching, my conversation with Neil was extremely difficult for me. It's hard to engage with someone when you know it's going to be painful and the stakes are high. It's hard to be in the middle of a conversation and feel that rush of adrenaline that makes you want to defend yourself or to fight back when someone blames, accuses, or judges you. But over the years I've learned that even though difficult conversations provide some of the greatest challenges, they can also create the most dramatic positive results. I've also learned that the same principles that work in dealing with people who are willing and aware also work in those challenging conversations with people who are unwilling and/or unaware.

Engagement Conversations

When a performer is unwilling and/or unaware of a performance issue, you're no longer dealing with a performer-driven conversation. You're dealing with a coach-driven conversation. In other words, you can't begin by drawing Goal, Reality, Options, and Way Forward out of your performer. Instead, *you* have to start. *You* own the agenda. It's *your* goal. You're trying to take this valued person from where he/she is to where *you* want him/her to go—which is basically to where he/she is willing to engage in a performer-driven conversation about the issue. Until the performer reaches that point, you're the one who's driving the conversation. If you were to begin a coach-driven discussion by asking, "What do you want from this discussion?" the performer would probably look at you as though you were crazy because *you'd* be the one asking to talk.

Engagement Conversations

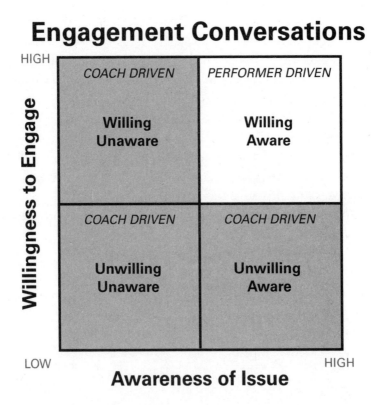

HIGH		
	COACH DRIVEN	*PERFORMER DRIVEN*
	Willing Unaware	**Willing Aware**
	COACH DRIVEN	*COACH DRIVEN*
	Unwilling Unaware	**Unwilling Aware**
LOW		**HIGH**

Willingness to Engage

Awareness of Issue

When a performer is willing, but unaware of the specific issue (upper-left-hand quadrant on the model), the discussion is generally not that difficult. Most of the time, you can simply go to the performer and say, "Hey, there's something we need to talk about" and he/she will say, "Sure. What is it?" And the person will engage. As a result, you can move immediately into a breakthrough conversation to deal with the performance issue.

However, when someone is unwilling to engage—aware or not (bottom two quadrants on the model)—the situation is different. The job of the coach in such situations is to get the performer's engagement—meaning *compliance* (at least) or *commitment* (at best)—to resolve the performance issue. And this is where we, as coaches, face our most difficult conversations.

What Makes Difficult Conversations "Difficult"

What makes difficult conversations "difficult" is interference. Think about the following scenarios:

- You're a manager. You have an employee who's performing poorly. He justifies his performance in his own mind and to others by blaming the system—and he doesn't want to talk about it. You don't want to write him up, but for the good of the company and the other members of the team, you can't let things continue as they are.

- You're a parent. In your opinion, your daughter's room is a pigsty. You've tried everything you can think of to encourage her to keep it clean—reasoning, cajoling, bribing, threatening, punishing—but nothing seems to work. For her sake (and yours), you feel strongly that she needs to shape up. But what you're doing is not solving the problem and is driving her farther and farther away.

- You're an employee. Your boss gives you an important assignment, but as you're carrying it out, you discover that he's planning on fulfilling part of it himself without even consulting you. And you're confident that what he's planning is going to have a significantly negative impact on the end result. You need to confront your boss, but you're reluctant—he's the one who controls your income and career opportunities.

- You need to give feedback to someone who is unaware that she's not performing as well as she thinks she is. But you're concerned about how to give that feedback in a way that she will actually hear and will not discourage her.

In situations such as these, ***the biggest challenge isn't the situation or the performer; it's your own interference***. And that changes your initial task as a coach.

In breakthrough conversations, it's the performer who has the interference, as shown in the first set of illustrations below. Your job as a coach is to help the performer clarify his/her thinking.

Breakthrough Conversations

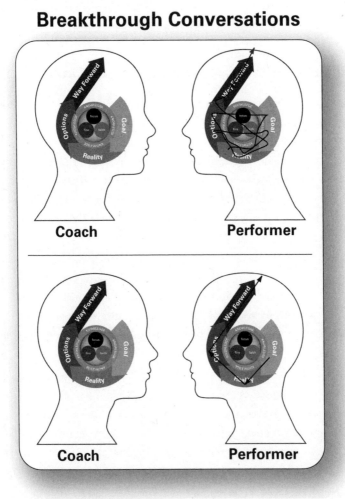

But in engagement conversations, you, the coach, often bring your own interference to the situation, as shown in the second set of illustrations. This creates problems for you, and it also creates additional interference for your performer. Only by getting rid of your own interference first can you effectively help others get rid of theirs. This is the same principle you see in operation when a flight attendant instructs you to put on your own oxygen mask before trying to help others put on theirs.

Engagement Conversations:
The Coach's Challenge

What Creates Interference for the Coach?

In difficult engagement conversations, a coach's interference comes primarily from two things:

1. Conflicting goals

- "My employee wants to keep doing what he's doing; I need him to improve."
- "My daughter wants to leave her room messy; I want her to keep it clean."

- "My boss wants to present part of the program; I want him to pull out so he doesn't ruin it."
- "My student wants to feel she's doing great; I need to tell her some things she needs to know to improve."

2. Fear of emotions and consequences

- "I don't want to offend this person."
- "This conversation will make her feel uncomfortable, which will make me feel uncomfortable, and I don't want to deal with that."
- "I'm afraid this person will push one of my buttons and I'll start responding emotionally instead of focusing on the issue."
- "This whole thing is so unpredictable. I have no idea what might happen or what I might say. I might even get flustered and lose track of the conversation—and that scares me."
- "I'm afraid to 'coach up' (to coach someone with more authority than I have) because if I'm honest about what I believe, my manager—or my leader or teacher or parent—might withhold privileges or resources, or even fire me."

Conflicting goals and fear of emotions or consequences can result in a coach's reluctance to even engage in the conversation. It can also trigger the "right/wrong" mechanism (if you're "right," that means I must be "wrong"), which leads to knee-jerk behavior and defensiveness that comes out in the tone, language, volume, and content of everything that's said.

THE "RIGHT/WRONG" MECHANISM

In order for me to be "right," you have to be "wrong." (You can't have a "right" without a "wrong"—one calls the other into being.) But being wrong is like death to an ego. So in order for your ego to survive, it cannot allow this. And if it isn't "wrong," then it must be "right."

So if you're "right," then I'm "wrong," which is death to my ego. Now my ego has to fight back and prove how "right" I am. So I start yelling at you (because we all know that "loud" means "right"). And if that doesn't work, I may even resort to violence to prove how "right" I am.

Clearly, this is an oversimplification. But the truth is that we typically fail to recognize how our struggle to be "right" affects another person—or even think about why that person might sincerely believe his/her point of view.

Understanding and addressing our own interference as coaches is critical because just as interference blocks the Faith, Fire, and Focus of the performer, it can also block the Faith, Fire, and Focus of the coach.

"I believe this conversation would really be hard." (Faith)
"I really don't want to engage." (Fire)
"All I can think about is avoiding this conversation." (Focus)

Nevertheless, we need to ask ourselves, "If I don't have this conversation now, what's going to happen or keep happening?" Often, as we compare the short-term pain of having a difficult conversation against the long-term pain of not having it, the disparity begins to change our Faith, Fire, and Focus.

"I believe that resolving the problem is more desirable than avoiding the short-term pain."
"I guess I really do want to engage in this conversation."
"So how can I best prepare for it and carry it out?"

Even in difficult conversations, we're still dealing with valued people— people who deserve to be treated with dignity and respect. (And if we don't see them that way, then *we're* the ones who need the coaching!) The process is still inside-out. Even though the conversation is "coach driven," it's still "performer focused." It's still about removing interference and helping people connect with their Faith, Fire, and Focus in a way that inspires their best.

Preparing for an Engagement Conversation

GROW can be enormously helpful in dealing with difficult coach-driven conversations in helping the coach prepare for the conversation and helping the coach actually conduct the conversation to engage the performer's buy-in. Before beginning an engagement conversation, it's helpful to take some time alone and ask yourself a few questions that will help you clarify your own thinking:

- What's my **Goal**? (To get the other person to buy into helping resolve the issue)

- What's the **Reality**?
  — What's been happening? Why has it been happening? Why is it a problem for me?
  — What are my beliefs about the person (Faith)? About the situation? Do I need help from someone else to clarify, challenge, or confirm my beliefs?
  — What's the level of my energy (Fire)? Is it positive or negative?
  — What am I paying attention to (Focus)? Am I more concerned about hearing myself or hearing the performer?
  — How might this issue appear from the performer's point of view?
  — What kind of language can I use to best communicate with the performer?
  — How might the performer respond in the conversation, and what reactions or emotions might that response evoke in me?
- What are my **Options**?
  — What could I do or say that would engage the performer's attention?
  — What choices do I have and what action will I take if the performer is not willing to engage?
  — What could I do if I feel myself getting drawn into an emotional black hole?
- What's my **Way Forward**?
  — How am I going to approach the conversation?
  — What are the specific words and phrases I plan to use?

IDENTIFY YOUR "BATNA"

In *Getting to Yes*, Roger Fisher, William Ury, and Bruce Patton of the Harvard Negotiation Project explain that in negotiating, it's important to identify your BATNA (Best Alternative to a Negotiated Agreement)—in other words, what course of action you will take if an agreement cannot be reached. This becomes your "contingency plan."

When you go into a difficult conversation with an employee, for example, you'll want to be clear about what your choices are if he/she refuses to engage in a performer-driven conversation. It might be that you will write up the situation and pass it on to superiors. It may be that the employee will be transferred or fired. It may be that legal action will be pursued.

If you are trying to engage in a difficult conversation with a teenager over handling responsibilities at home, your contingency plan may be that you will no longer provide money for projects or recreation or permit him/her to use the family car.

The person you're working with may end up being cooperative and you may never need to bring up your BATNA. But if you make your decision ahead of time, it will decrease interference. It will also enable you to evaluate the progress of the conversation against that default outcome and, if necessary, help the performer do the same.

Actually crafting a conversation in advance can help you crystallize your thinking and eliminate much of the interference you would otherwise encounter.

Once you plan the conversation, role-playing it with someone else ahead of time allows you to practice with and refine the language. It also allows you to practice dealing with conflicts or emotions. When someone goes on the defensive and attacks you verbally in a conversation, it's usually not about you personally; it's about that individual not wanting to deal with something that's uncomfortable or even painful. But that's often hard to recognize in the moment. If you're not prepared, it's easy to react to the attack and start to justify and defend yourself—in which case, you won't be able to really "hear" or help that person at all. By dealing with your own potential conflicts and emotions in advance, there's less chance they will become a distraction in the actual conversation.

Of course, there's a good possibility that the actual conversation will go differently than you plan. But even if it does, the effort you put into planning—particularly in clarifying your Goal, identifying the actions you will take if you don't get agreement, and dealing with your own conflicts and emotions—will put you in a far better position to respond effectively during the conversation.

It's not always possible to plan a difficult conversation in advance. Sometimes situations arise that need to be handled immediately. You might be in the middle of a breakthrough conversation and suddenly realize that what the performer (the employee, child, spouse, student) wants to do is not

> **In preparing for battle I have always found that plans are useless, but planning is indispensable.**
>
> DWIGHT D. EISENHOWER, former U.S. president and Supreme Commander of the Allied Expeditionary Force, World War II

acceptable. Suddenly you find yourself in an unplanned engagement conversation with no opportunity to prepare. Learning to recognize the "cues" on page 81 will enable you to quickly and confidently shift into the appropriate mode. However, most of the time you *will* be able to prepare for difficult conversations, including going through all the elements of GROW. And doing so can significantly increase your performance as a coach. If you think about it, practice is vital to any high-quality performance. No top athlete, musician, or other performer would even think of trying to perform without it.

Using GROW helped me as I prepared to have the difficult conversation with Neil described at the beginning of this chapter. The questions helped me to be clear about my Goal—to get Neil to engage in a conversation to address the issues that were causing his poor performance and personal pain. They helped me identify the Realities that would impact the conversation—the consequences of his behavior, his reticent nature, his tendency to lash out, his sensitivity to the nature of the problems he was dealing with. They helped me recognize the Realities of my Faith (about Neil as a friend and as a valuable contributor in the organization), my Fire (my energy about resolving this issue), and my Focus (to resolve this in a way that would bring positive long-term results for Neil, our relationship, and the organization). They helped me think of Options—of different ways I might be able to engage Neil's attention and commitment. They helped identify my contingency plan (to either get Neil to engage or be dragged off by the police) and determine my Way Forward.

Crafting the conversation in advance enabled me to imagine and deal with emotions and challenges ahead of time, which helped me remain calm when they actually surfaced in the conversation. It also helped me to think about the process and the language I could use to best communicate with Neil.

NEURO-LINGUISTIC PROGRAMMING

According to Neuro-Linguistic Programming (NLP) developers Richard Bandler and John Grinder, people have one of three dominant modes of processing the world—visual (sight), auditory (sound), or kinesthetic (touch). Understanding and matching the mode of the person with whom you're having a conversation can significantly enhance communication.

For example, if the person is primarily visual, you might use phrases such as "I see what you mean," "I get the picture," or "I understand your point of view."

If you're talking with someone who is primarily auditory, you might say things such as, "I hear what you're saying" or "That sounds good to me."

In conversation with a person who is primarily kinesthetic, you might say, "Okay, I grasp the idea" or "I've got a handle on what you mean."

As Bandler and Grinder point out, there are various ways to determine the primary mode of a person, but one of the quickest and easiest is to simply listen to the person's language. Notice whether the person uses primarily seeing, hearing, or touching words.

Conducting an Engagement Conversation

Once you've prepared for an engagement conversation, your next task is to actually conduct the conversation. Keep in mind that your Goal is to engage someone in a performer-driven conversation to resolve an issue. Your problem is that your performer doesn't share that goal. He/she is either unaware of the problem or is unwilling to talk about it—or both. So there's a gap between your Goal and Reality and your performer's Goal and Reality.

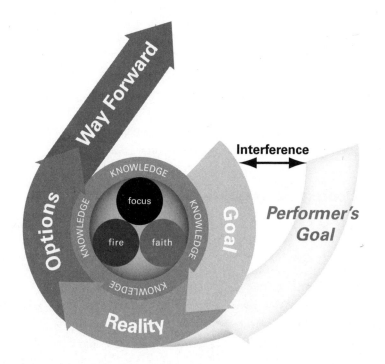

If your performer is willing but unaware, you might only need to share your Goal ("I'd like to involve you in a discussion of how to solve a problem") and Reality ("The reports I've been getting from you don't have all the information I need"). At that point, the person might say, "Wow! I had no idea. Sure, I'd be happy to talk about that." And that would be all that's needed. The gap would be closed, and you could shift immediately to a breakthrough conversation with the shared goal of resolving the issue.

However, if the person is unwilling, you may need to move to Options and clarify everyone's choices ("We can talk about this now, or we can talk about it tomorrow"; "If we don't talk about it, this is what I'm going to have to do"). With a clearer awareness of the options and consequences, the person may choose at that point to buy in, closing the gap and allowing you to move to the performer-driven model. If the person still doesn't buy in, you may need to act on *your* Way Forward or contingency plan. In that case, you have the confidence of knowing that you've given your performer the best possible opportunity to make a knowledgeable choice, and that confidence will decrease the interference you might otherwise feel in moving ahead.

Recognizing this gap and knowing you may have to move to your contingency plan highlight the importance of two of the preparation questions on pages 111–112:

- What could I do or say that would engage the performer's attention?
- What choices do I have and what action will I take if the performer is not willing to engage?

Clarity on those two issues will remove much of the fear of initiating the conversation and of being able to handle whatever happens.

"The Monthly Reports Are Coming in Late"

Let's take a look now at the first of the four scenarios introduced on page 107—a manager with an employee who is performing poorly and doesn't want to talk about it. The following dialogue is based on an actual conversation and incorporates the main elements of many similar conversations.

The situation is that Steve, a supervisor at a chemical company, has not been a great performer. He has an attitude and style that make him hard to manage—so hard, in fact, that his previous managers have given him good appraisals so that he would be promoted or transferred because it was easier for them to do that than to try to "fix" him. Brynn is Steve's new manager. She's been in the job for six months, and for the last three, Steve has turned in monthly reports up to a week late—each time with an excuse. Brynn is aware of Steve's history, and she's decided it's time to do something about the situation. She's already gone through the GROW process herself to prepare for this conversation and decrease her own interference. Her Goal now is to get Steve to engage in resolving the issue. In accomplishing that goal, Brynn again uses the GROW process. Although there is some back-and-forth movement between Goal, Reality, and Options (which is typical in difficult conversations), the general flow is still the same.

In using the process, Brynn focuses on a few critical variables that reduce interference in coach-driven conversations. These variables include the following:

- **Sharing intent** (which removes the fear of the unknown)
- **Showing respect** (listening empathically, giving choices, and asking permission)
- **Telling your truth** (sharing your perspective honestly and clearly)
- **Remaining open to new information** (acknowledging that you may not have all the relevant facts, and that you might revise your perspective if you did)
- **Using baby steps** (creating small wins wherever possible; also creating a series of small "yeses" that make it more difficult for the performer to say "no")

Addressing these critical variables not only reduces interference for the performer; focusing on them also reduces interference for the coach. Now let's see how Brynn handles her challenging engagement conversation with Steve.

> Brynn: Steve, I'm struggling with a problem, and I'd really like to get your help with it. [*By acknowledging her ownership of the problem, Brynn immediately reduces some interference. It's not "you have a problem" or even "we have a problem"; it's "I have a problem" (and her problem is getting Steve to buy in). Also, because it's her problem, it's less of a threat.*] Can we talk about it now? [*Asking permission (i.e.,*

giving Steve a choice) makes the situation less threatening and further reduces interference.]

Steve: [*belligerently*] Why me? How can I help you with your problems? [***Obviously, Steve falls into the "unwilling" category.***]

Brynn: Well, this problem involves my perception of your performance with the monthly reports. [***Brynn is increasing the challenge, but only one small step at a time to minimize interference.***]

Steve: Oh, I get it. So it's time to chew out Steve again. Look, Brynn, I haven't got time for this. I've got work to do. [***Steve goes on the offensive as a form of defense.***]

Brynn: Steve, the last thing I want to do is chew you out. But I do want to try and find a way to resolve this. What I'd like to do is to share my data with you and then understand how the whole thing looks to you. If I'm accurate, all I want to do is work with you to find a way to resolve it in the most painless way possible for both of us. And if I'm not accurate, I'll get out of your hair and stop wasting your time. [***Clarifying a win-win Goal and process for resolution up front—and also acknowledging that her perception may not be accurate and she's willing to change—further eliminates interference.***] So, can we talk about it? [***Here's another request for permission and buy-in.***]

Steve: Look, you know what our work schedule's like out there. You know how many things we're trying to deal with. [*sigh*] How long is this going to take?

Brynn: I would think . . . maybe fifteen minutes.

Steve: [*reluctantly*] All right. Let's go ahead and take care of it now. So what did Steve do this time? [***Notice how he's playing the victim. Steve's showing signs of beginning to buy in.***]

Brynn: Well, Steve, I've been here for six months. You've been here twenty years. You've had great appraisals. But suddenly, the last three months, the reports have come in sometimes up to a week late. And I don't understand why. [***This is a clear statement of the issue, but the problem still belongs to the coach—"I don't understand."***]

Steve: Look, Brynn, I don't want to sit here and get chewed out for something that's not my fault. I've been telling management around here for months— these people are just incompetent. I'm doing their work for them. And I don't know what else to do. They turn stuff in that's late and inaccurate, and I have to redo it. [***Note Steve's effort to redirect responsibility for his performance.***]

Brynn: So first of all, we agree that the reports are coming in late. [***Notice the*** *use of empathic listening (future uses marked with an asterisk°)— also verbal recognition of an area of agreement (a small win-win).]*

Steve: Yeah.

Brynn: And you're saying the reason is because the people you've got are incompetent and they hand the work in late to you, and then you have to redo it. [*empathic listening*]

Steve: That's right. I've got to redo their figures and recompute them, so I've got my work to do and then their work to do as well. I end up babysitting them all the time.

Brynn: It sounds like this is as frustrating to you as it is to me. [*°Empathic listening—note how it includes paying attention to emotions and body language as well as words.*]

Steve: It sure is. I don't like being chewed out for something like this. It's not really my issue. It's not my fault.

Brynn: Steve, I want to say again, I'm not trying to chew you out. All I want to do here is find a way to solve this so that it doesn't drive us both crazy. [**Here Brynn is reaffirming a win-win Goal.**]

Steve: [*interrupting*] Look, you really want to solve it?

Brynn: I *really* want to solve it.

Steve: Okay, fire the whole bunch of them. Get somebody in there that can do the job. If they don't want to do the job now, get somebody in there who does. I only had two good people before, and you took them away. So let's get somebody in there who knows what they're doing. Besides, the workload has doubled over the last six months, so let's double the staff so we can get the analysis in when it's supposed to be in. [**It would be easy for Brynn to react emotionally or to be judgmental about Steve's sweeping and unrealistic proposal. But that response would not engage Steve's Faith, Fire, and Focus or improve his performance.**]

Brynn: Okay, so I think I'm hearing some more information now. One thing is, there's more to do than ever before. [*°empathic listening—no judgment, no emotional reaction*]

Steve: That's right.

Brynn: And I took your two best people away and transferred them. [*°empathic listening*]

Steve: Yeah.

Brynn: Okay. And so your solution, as I understand it, would be to fire everybody right now and then rehire. [*°empathic listening*]

Steve: Yeah.

Brynn: Now, I certainly agree with one piece of what you've said, Steve, and that is there's more to do now than ever before. [*Again, Brynn is acknowledging areas of agreement—another little win-win.*] I think that's something everybody wrestles with because business is different. But I see other pieces of what you've said differently. [*Brynn is also acknowledging their differences, but without debating them or getting into a right/wrong conversation.*] You know, I'm not in a position to fire everybody, and even if I were, I don't think I would right now because I suspect that if you and I were to put some quality thought into this together, we could find a way to deal with it without having to do that. And that's all I want to do—to spend some quality time with you trying to figure out how to do it. [*She's reclarifying the Goal.*] So what do you think? [*Here's another request for buy-in.*]

Steve: [*reluctantly*] Well, I guess so. Nothing's going to change unless we change the situation out there. [*Steve's beginning to accept responsibility for the problem.*] [*pause*] So how long is it going to take again?

Brynn: I don't know—fifteen, maybe thirty, minutes. And look, if now's not the right time, let's do it later on today. [*This shows Brynn's willingness to be flexible, to let Steve decide when to meet.*]

Steve: Sheila and I have been working on a project all day. Let me call her and tell her that I can't meet until two o'clock. She can start working on some of the preliminary stuff, and then I'll come in right after lunch. We can take care of it then.

Brynn: Great. Look, Steve, I really appreciate it. [*This affirms Steve's decision to engage.*]

Steve: Okay.

Brynn: Thanks.

Steve: Sure.

Notice how the conversation with Steve becomes less threatening and his defenses lower as Brynn focuses on the critical variables:

Share your intent:
"I'd like to share my data . . ."
"I'd like to understand how the whole thing looks to you . . ."
"If I'm accurate, I want to find a way to resolve the problem in the most painless way possible for both of us (win-win) . . . If I'm not accurate, I'll get out of your hair . . ."

Show respect:
- *Listen empathically:*

    "You're saying the reason why the reports are coming in late is because . . ."

    "It sounds like this is as frustrating to you as it is to me . . ."

    "So your solution is to fire everybody right now and then rehire . . ."
- *Give choices:*

    "If now's not the right time, let's do it later on today."
- *Ask permission:*

    "Can we talk about it now?"

    "All I want to do is spend some quality time with you trying to figure out how to do this. So what do you think?"

Tell your truth:

"The reports are coming in late and I don't understand why . . ."

"I see other pieces of what you've said differently."

"I'm not in a position to fire everybody, and even if I were, I don't think I would . . ."

Remain open to new information:

"Here are my perceptions, which may or may not be accurate. Let's talk about it."

"I'd like to understand how the whole thing looks to you . . ."

"Okay, so I think I'm hearing some more information now . . ."

Use baby steps:
- *Create small wins wherever possible.*

    "So we agree that the reports are coming in late."

    "I agree with one piece of what you've said—there's more to do now than ever before."

    "The conversation should only take fifteen, maybe thirty, minutes."
- *Create a series of small "yeses" that make it more difficult to say "no."*

    "I'm wrestling with a problem, and I'd really like to get your help with it. Can we talk about it now?"

    "If I'm not accurate, hey, I'll get out of your hair and stop wasting your time. So, can we talk about it?

In the end, the inside-out approach brings Steve to the point of buy-in, where he is willing to interact. He may not be exactly ecstatic about the prospect, but at least his resentment has been defused and he agrees to meet and try to work out a solution to the problem. He agrees to take some responsibility for and ownership of the issue.

In contrast, consider the likely results if Brynn had used the typical outside-in approach: "Ready . . . fire . . . aim!" This is what happens when we assume we know what's wrong and come in shooting from the hip with both barrels loaded. The effort is not to understand or to get buy-in; it's to get compliance. We may end up with compliance, but we won't end up with commitment. And instead of being released, Faith, Fire, and Focus will be further blocked by increased interference.

"We Can't Talk—I've Got Work to Do!"

What would have happened if the situation had been even more intense? What if Steve had been insubordinate and refused to even engage? Let's look at what might happen in this more challenging scenario.

> Brynn: Steve, I'm struggling with a problem at the moment that I'd really like your help with. Can we spend some time talking about it now please?
>
> Steve: No, we can't, Brynn. I've got work to do. [*Steve flatly refuses to engage.*]
>
> Brynn: Steve, the problem I'm struggling with involves you. It's about how I'm viewing your performance on these monthly reports. [*This gets the issue immediately out in the open.*]
>
> Steve: Look, you want to solve the problem? Let me get back to work. That's where I need to be—working out there. I haven't got time to sit and go through all this crap.
>
> Brynn: Steve, I can't solve this without you. I need to be able to talk with you about it.
>
> Steve: I'm sorry. But what can I do? I haven't got time for this.
>
> Brynn: You know, Steve, what I wanted to do was to work with you and find a way to resolve this in the most painless way for both of us. But if you and I can't even talk, I don't know what else to do other than write to you. And you know what happens with that—it goes on file and there are consequences for both of us. [*This is where Brynn shares her contingency plan if Steve doesn't buy in (see pages 117–120).*] And that's the last thing I want to have happen. That's why I'm saying, can we talk about it now or sometime today? [*Brynn is not judging (good/bad/right/wrong); she's clarifying intent, choices, consequences, and what's nonnegotiable. Also, she's once again asking permission.*]

Steve: [*resentfully*] What choice do I have? [**Steve again plays the victim. Brynn knows he needs to understand that he does have choices, but his choices have consequences.**]

Brynn: Well, you have at least two—you can talk about it or you can not talk about it. I'm saying, "Give *me* another choice." I don't want to do the stuff that starts creating more hassle for both of us. [**Brynn lets Steve know that accountability for at least deciding whether or not to engage in a conversation—and the consequences of that decision—are in his hands.**]

Steve: [*after a pause*] Well, all right. Let me talk to Sheila and tell her we can't meet until two, and then we'll just talk about it after lunch, I guess.

Brynn: All right. Is one o'clock okay?

Steve: Yeah.

Brynn: Thanks, Steve.

Steve: Okay.

When Steve says, "I'm not even going to discuss this," it changes the Reality—and therefore the Options—for Brynn. Steve remains unwilling, and this is where the contingency plan comes in. Brynn says, "I'm trying to resolve this in the easiest way for both of us, but if you won't even discuss this with me, then I've got no choice other than to write you up, and it's the last thing I want to do." Because of her preparation for this conversation, she's clear in her own mind ahead of time that this is where she will go if Steve won't engage. She's clear about it in her conversation with Steve, and she's also clear with him that this is not where she *wants* to go. Her desire is to go to a breakthrough conversation to resolve the issue. But if Steve refuses, she clearly tells him what the consequence will be.

Confronted with this contingency plan, Steve goes on the offensive in an interesting way by playing the victim. "What choice do I have?" He's inferring that Brynn is denying him his right as an employee and possibly as a human being. She helps him understand that he has two choices. "You can discuss it or you can refuse. I'm saying give me another choice because if you refuse, then this is what I will do." It's blunt, but it's respectful. Steve is still in control.

Eventually (though reluctantly), Steve buys in. He decides he's *willing* to talk. And that willingness shifts the conversation to a different level. He may still struggle. He may still be stuck in stories of blaming and accusing others for poor performance. But the door is now open to explore together the Goals, Realities, and Options that lead to an effective Way Forward. And during the course of that conversation, Brynn would not only be able to listen empathically and reflect understanding of Steve's perspective in an affirming way but when the time is right, she would also be able to offer additional perspective that might help change Steve's limiting beliefs.

When someone with an attitude and performance record like Steve's gets turned around, it not only benefits the individual; it also benefits the organization that doesn't have to pay to replace him/her. And it adds to the joy and satisfaction of the coach as well. Again, while these conversations can be very difficult, they are also extremely high leverage.

Other Applications of the Engagement Conversation

Let's now look at the other three scenarios introduced on page 107. These scenarios may give you additional insight as to how the principles can be applied when you become involved in any kind of engagement conversation.

Engaging a Child in Cleaning Her Room

One dad shared with me an ongoing challenge he and his wife had in trying to get their ten-year-old daughter to keep her room clean. According to him, their efforts sometimes led to "vigorous discussions" and disciplinary actions, which were frustrating to everyone. Finally, he decided to coach his daughter through the process.

He began by asking for her help in solving a problem he had been dealing with. When she agreed to help, he told her what the problem was and explained his perception of the situation. At first, she was skeptical, thinking this would be another of her dad's "do this or else" edicts. But as the discussion progressed, she learned that he was really interested in her perception of the situation and her ideas on how to solve the problem. Her attitude changed, and she was willing to participate in the discussion. In the course of the conversation, this dad learned that his daughter perceived her parents as being way too fussy with their expectations for her room. She also felt that maintaining a neat and orderly room would take away from her limited free time. Nonetheless, she did agree that maintaining some standard of cleanliness would work to everyone's benefit, including hers.

At that point, the discussion shifted to how they could address the problem they both now wanted to solve. When the dad asked the daughter for her ideas, she suggested creating a daily checklist to remind her of specific tasks she needed to do to keep her room from becoming a disaster area. Her dad asked her to suggest the items that should appear on the list, and much to his surprise, her suggestions went beyond what he thought she would be willing to do on a daily basis. The daughter also suggested that a financial incentive wouldn't hurt, so he agreed to a little extra weekly allowance when each day's checklist was satisfactorily completed. This father said,

> So far the new system is working as designed. We've seen a significant improvement in the general condition of our daughter's room. I think one of the strengths of this approach is that it helps parents and children solve problems without the adversarial conflict that hurts relationships. In particular, it points to the value of allowing the other person to have input and to share ownership in the solution.

There are key turning points in inside-out coaching conversations that make a huge difference in engaging a performer's Faith, Fire, and Focus. In this experience, one such turning point occurred when the daughter realized her dad was genuinely trying to solve a problem, not just pull rank or "preach" to her. Another was when she realized he sincerely valued her input and was open to her suggestions—including the increase in allowance. The father had some important turning points that engaged his Faith, Fire, and Focus as well. One was in the very beginning when he realized he could substitute the inside-out approach for his outside-in approach to parenting. Another was when he realized that his daughter had come up with a list that was more detailed than he would have thought—probably more detailed than he would have come up with—and that she had more Fire about following up on it because she had invested in creating it.

These kinds of turning points open the door to Ways Forward that are truly win-win and viable, and they can happen in conversations with teenagers about almost anything—repeated failure to come home on time, playing music that causes distress, dressing in a way that causes concern, "hanging out" with kids that seem to have a negative influence, or becoming involved in behaviors that are counterproductive.

It's my experience that the more parents use the inside-out approach in dealing with issues with their kids, the more likely the kids are to initiate breakthrough conversations on all kinds of issues of their own—how to do better in school, how to deal with concerns with their friends, what activities they should become involved in or drop, or which college to attend. The nature of this approach helps keep the door to communication with teenagers open at this challenging time in their lives.

Coaching Up

Ron, a mid-level manager, shared an experience he had in "coaching up"—a term used to describe the process of addressing an issue with someone in a position of real or perceived authority above you, such as a boss who controls your income, an instructor who's used to telling you what to do, or a parent with whom you've had a deferential relationship for years. For many people, the idea of coaching up creates so much interference that it completely blocks Faith and Fire and causes a shift in Focus to avoid the conversation. But coaching up conversations are often critical to enduring, high-performance, and positive relationships.

In this particular situation, Ron had the task of putting together a team of twelve facilitators for a large leadership development program to be rolled out in twelve cities over a period of four months. He had done considerable evaluating and interviewing and was getting fairly close to finalizing the team when a couple of the other project members came to him and said, "Are you aware that Mark (Ron's boss) is thinking he's going to be one of the facilitators?" This took Ron completely by surprise. In his opinion, Mark was a great boss, but he came nowhere near meeting the fifteen criteria required of facilitators.

At first, Ron didn't believe it. But then he noticed that Mark was starting to make travel arrangements for the sessions they were doing. At that point, Ron decided he needed to prepare for what could be a difficult conversation with his boss. Ron attended two or three of Mark's presentations and took detailed notes. He tried to decide what the potential actions would be if Mark didn't buy in. Obviously, he couldn't fire his boss. He decided the only thing he really could do was say to him, "Look, you said I was the project leader. You put me in charge of making the final call on these facilitators. I'm going to ask you to not be on the facilitation team." But Ron was hoping he would never have to say those words.

After spending some time crafting what he wanted to say, Ron went to his boss and said, "Hey, Mark, when you have a few minutes, I have something I want to run by you with regard to the facilitation team. I'd like to get your perspective." Mark replied, "Well, now's a good time." So they went to the nearest empty meeting room and sat down. The conversation went something like this:

Ron: Mark, what I'd like to do is share my perspective of your desire to be on the facilitation team. Is this still a good time to talk?

Mark: Well, yeah. Sure.

Ron: What I'd like to do is to share with you what I'm seeing and hearing. Then I want to get your take on it. If we're on the same page, then we can talk about how we move forward. If we're not on the same page, then I need you to help me fill in the gaps—to tell me what's missing. Is this still a good time to talk?

Mark: Yeah, it's okay.

Ron: All right. I've heard from a couple of people that you've made some travel reservations, and your assumption is that you will be part of the facilitators' team. Is that right?

Mark: Yes it is.

Ron: I've also put out some criteria for this job. It's my perspective that you only meet three out of the fifteen criteria and here's why. I've watched a couple of your facilitated sessions. You said more than twenty "um's" in the first half hour. During a facilitated piece, you asked no open-ended questions. You looked up at the ceiling twenty times. You made very little eye contact with the audience. You spoke eighty percent of the time, and the group spoke twenty percent of the time. [*He paused for a moment.*] Now that's my perception. Am I on or am I off here?

Mark: [*a bit nervously*] Ron, with regard to most of what you've shared, you're right on. I've heard that feedback before.

Ron: Look, Mark. I want you to know that this is really hard for me. I care about you as a friend and as a colleague, and I wouldn't consider myself much of a friend if I didn't share this with you. So we do agree that you don't meet all the criteria for a facilitator?

Mark: Yes. You know, even when I think a little about the other things you mentioned, I'm probably there with you.

Ron: Good. So how might we move forward to identify your role for the project?

Mark: Well, I think I'm just really wrestling with what my role is.

Ron: Okay. So really, the Goal is to try and figure out your role. Is that right?

Mark: That's right.

Ron: Would you like my help in processing through it?

Mark: Sure. I'd really appreciate that.

So then they moved into a GROW discussion about Mark's role. It was a less stressful and a more focused discussion. The action outcome was that Mark would stay behind at the corporate office as the point person in case they had problems or needs while out on the road. He felt that was something that he would enjoy and that would be a good role for him. Ron later said:

> In retrospect, that was probably one of the toughest conversations I've ever had to have. After all, Mark signs my checks and gives me my performance reviews. But it actually turned out great. Bottom line, Mark's really a talented individual and I learned a lot from him as a boss. I just think that since nobody had ever given him any feedback about his facilitating skills, he simply assumed that he was doing great and that this was a good role for him. This was the first time someone had shared specific feedback on his ability to deliver and present content.

As Ron discovered (and as is frequently the case), the experience itself was not as uncomfortable as he had thought it was going to be. This was due, in good part, to his careful research and planning, which allowed him to craft what to Focus on in the conversation and identify his contingency plan. In addition to helping him reduce his own interference, this approach also guided his choice of words to help him change the Focus and reduce the interference of his boss, thereby enabling him to engage his boss in a breakthrough conversation to resolve the issue.

Giving Feedback

In the process of taking valued people from where they are to where they want to go, we often need to give performers feedback to help them become aware of an issue or an opportunity to improve their performance. Until we can help performers increase their awareness of the gap between what they *think* they're doing and what they're *actually* doing, they can't take responsibility for doing things differently.

For most people, feedback is a paradox. Most of us say we want it and on the surface will tell you it's valuable. But we're often anxious about receiving it. The reason is that rather than understanding feedback as a perception of data, many of us see it as just another name for criticism delivered in a sensitive way. It creates interference because we hear the information as judgment. Our reaction is to discount, avoid, or become defensive when people tell us what we "should" have done.

To understand the dynamics of feedback, imagine that you are the navigational component and I'm the steering component in the autopilot of an airplane. If the plane starts to tip slightly to the left, you say, "Alan, you're banking to the left."

I reply, "Thank you very much," and I course correct.

If the plane starts to tip slightly to the right, you say, "Alan, you're banking to the right."

I say, "Thank you very much," and course correct.

If the nose of the plane starts to go down, you say, "Alan, your nose is dropping."

Again I say, "Thank you very much" and course correct.

Throughout the flight, you're giving me immediate nonstop feedback. And this feedback enables me to stay on course so that we arrive at our destination safely and on time. But when human beings try to do the same thing, this is what tends to happen:

"Alan, you're banking to the left."
"Thank you very much."
"Alan, you're banking to the right."
"Yeah . . . well, okay."
"Alan, your nose is dropping."
"You know what? All you ever do is criticize me!"

I'm not hearing this as feedback anymore. I'm hearing it as criticism. And that plays into my greatest fear—my fear of being judged. So now my defenses are up. My Faith, Fire, and Focus are being threatened. I'm in watch-out mode. I'm no longer listening to what you have to say. But what would happen in an airplane if the two components in the computer didn't listen to each other? Crash and burn. You probably know people whose careers have crashed and burned because they cut themselves off from feedback. They never reached the level of performance they needed to reach, and they never under-stood why because they couldn't deal with feedback.

In its pure form, feedback is merely data. And this data is what gives us the ability to recognize the gap between what we think we do and what we actually do. The key to giving and receiving feedback effectively is to use the principles of the inside-out approach.

My friend, business consultant JoAnn Kailikea, shares a helpful way to visualize why these principles are important and how to apply them. You can validate the usefulness of this visualization through your own experience. Envision a meeting between you and me, and pretend I'm your manager. You're holding a glass and I have a pitcher of water. The water represents the feedback I want to give you—feedback I am convinced would be enormously helpful to you in your role. Now I know that for feedback to be useful, it has to be timely and relevant. Metaphorically, we call that "close to home." So I'm going to ask you to hold the glass as close to your heart as you can get it. However, you already have quite a few ideas in mind that you believe will help you improve, so your glass is not empty. In fact, it's nearly full. But I'm so ex-cited to give you this feedback that I don't really notice that, and I'm getting ready to pour.

So what do you do? You're holding a nearly full glass of water close to your heart. You realize that as soon as I start to pour my feedback into your glass, it's going to run out over the top of the glass and spill all over your clothes. So you quickly move the glass away from your chest—in fact, you move it as far away as you possibly can so you won't get wet. And what's the result? Whatever feedback I give you is *not* going to be close to your heart (not as timely or rel-evant). Then I start to pour. I say, "I think you've done a terrific job with these things." I keep pouring. "And I'm really proud about the way you did this." I keep pouring. "But I'd do this a little differently . . . and I'd change the way you do that." By this time, water is going all over the place. What's the prob-lem? I'm giving you too much, and you're not even getting it. In fact, you're drowning.

Giving feedback in this way is outside-in. It's not performer centered; it's coach centered. And the feedback doesn't help you. In fact, it creates interfer-ence, which begins to block your Faith, Fire, and Focus. In addition, it actually gets in the way of our relationship and my ability to help. It also creates an-other problem. As the rest of the team watches what's happening, they're making the decision to never come to me for feedback. You often see this happen in organizations, and it feeds the reality that people don't leave organizations; they leave their leaders—many of whom are drowning their peers with feedback.

The inside-out approach, on the other hand, keeps more of the ownership for what happened and what will happen with the performer. It makes a person responsible for thinking through and evaluating his/her own performance. Imagine me coming to you and saying up front, "I have some feedback I think would be useful to you. Would you like to hear it?" By asking that question, I'm in effect asking if you would be willing to engage in a breakthrough conversation around a shared Goal: working together to create a plan to improve your performance. If you're not willing (unwilling and unaware on the Coaching Conversation model), we may need to move into a conversation similar to those Brynn had with Steve earlier in this chapter in order to create engagement. But if you are willing (willing but unaware on the model) or once you become willing, we'd move into a breakthrough conversation and I'd ask you to share your Reality and Options. In other words, *I ask you to empty your glass first.* The way I do this is by asking you three questions:

> "So that I don't tell you things you already know, you tell me:
>> What do you think worked?
>> Where did you get stuck?
>> What would you do differently next time?"

I'm not distracting you with my judgment; I'm helping you tap into your own inner wisdom. I'm helping you Focus on a few simple things that will increase your awareness of your own experience and help you to learn. I'm encouraging you to take responsibility for self-assessing. By the time you share your perspective on these questions, your glass is empty and you're ready to receive whatever additional perspective I have to share. So I then share my Reality and Options. I start out by affirming those things you said that I could agree with. Then I ask if you'd like to hear my observations. If you say "yes," I share my perspective on the same three questions I asked you. I tell you what I saw that worked, where I thought you might have gotten stuck, and what I think you might do differently to be more effective next time. I keep whatever feedback I give you immediate, specific, and nonjudgmental.

GIVING FEEDBACK INSIDE-OUT

Step 1: Ask permission.
"I have some feedback I think would be useful to you. Would you like to hear it?
Step 2: Empty the performer's glass first.
So that I don't tell you things you already know, tell me:
What worked?
Where did you get stuck?
What would you do differently next time?
Step 3: Endorse what you agree with, then offer your observations.
Would you like to hear my observations?
Step 4: Build on what the performer said.
What worked? (Celebrate the performer's success.)
Where did you get stuck? (Avoid "failure" discussion.)
What would you do differently next time? (Identify actions.)
Keep feedback immediate, specific, and nonjudgmental.

After we both share our perceptions of Reality and Options, we might then brainstorm together regarding additional options. Then you would choose a Way Forward that tapped into your Faith and Fire.

Sharing feedback in this way shows respect for your own inner wisdom. It reduces interference, avoids wasting time on things you already know, and enables you to "hear" information that may be critical to your performance.

The Most Common Mistakes

As people work to integrate the inside-out approach in conducting engagement conversations, the most common mistakes they experience are these:

1. Failure to Plan. When we neglect to plan before engaging in difficult conversations, we tend to fall into the "Ready . . . fire . . . aim!" approach. An example of this is when we yell at our children, repeatedly, over the same issue. (And we think *they're* stupid?) In all my experience, I have yet to find a child who will say, "Oh, thank you! I do so much better when you yell at me." I also have yet to find a situation in which yelling actually accomplishes what a parent thinks it does!

The reason we get into "Ready . . . fire . . . aim!" is basically interference. We become frustrated, and yelling seems to be the quickest way to let our frustration out. Planning helps us avoid the frustration. We go through the GROW process ourselves to be clear on our Goal (to engage the person in a breakthrough conversation), our Reality, our Options (including which actions we would be willing to take if there's no resolution), and our Way Forward. We anticipate what interference we might encounter and determine how we will handle it.

Again, just as no self-respecting athlete would ever go into his/her most difficult challenge without thorough and careful preparation, whenever possible we should never engage in difficult conversations without carefully and thoroughly planning first.

2. Failure to Listen. Clearly, listening is critical. Not only does it help the other person feel respected and understood; it's also a powerful way for us as coaches to create Focus and reduce our own interference. When we don't listen, we don't show respect. In the language of leadership expert Stephen R. Covey, we deprive people of "psychological air,"[1] and when people are suddenly deprived of air (physical or psychological), the only thing they focus on is getting it. Not listening also causes us to miss getting vital information we need to come up with viable solutions. In addition, there's no way we can play back to people their own thinking or help them put it under a microscope and examine it if we don't listen and help them give expression to their thoughts.

However, listening is not always an easy thing to do—particularly if we're not in the habit of doing it. And even when we *think* we're listening, most of us would be very surprised if we could literally watch ourselves in the interaction and see how little real listening is taking place. One client I worked with said: "I always thought I was a great listener. But when I put the GROW process into actual practice and stayed very attentive to it, I discovered I was much more anxious to share my opinion than listen. It was almost comical when I realized just how much I was biting my tongue in order to listen more."

Another person told me that the most helpful thing about using GROW was that it forced her to "shut up." She said this insight created a profound revelation for her because she began to see how often she had been thinking about what she was going to say and worrying about telling her stories in the right order instead of really listening. She had created a rapport with her performers, but they hadn't gone anywhere with it because instead of helping them release their Faith, Fire, and Focus, she had basically just been using up time.

Realizing that we probably aren't listening as effectively as we could is the first step to improving our own performance as a coach. From that point, helpful things we can do include the following:

— Making the conscious decision in each interaction to set aside our own agenda/experience and focus on seeing the world through the performer's point of view.

— Consistently reflecting back what the performer is saying in our own words ("So what I'm hearing you say is . . .") and noticing how often the performer says things such as, "Yes," "That's right," or "No, that's not what I meant."

— Observing others in coaching situations (or even ourselves in video-recorded interactions) and asking, "Whose needs are being addressed here—the performer's or the coach's?"

The better we get at truly listening, the better we're able to help others raise their performance and help ourselves, as coaches, raise our own.

3. Failure to Follow the Process. A common reason people don't use GROW effectively is that they don't follow the process. And the most common reason they don't follow the process is habit. They've responded to others in their own particular style for so long that they fall into it naturally without even thinking. They do what's comfortable rather than what works. The key here is to keep your goal of actually helping the person in mind and being very clear on what creates results—and what doesn't.

Another reason is that people get emotionally caught up in what the person they're trying to help is saying. If you're trying to help someone who's struggling with how to stop a five-year-old from throwing temper tantrums—and you think, "Wow! I'm having that same problem with my five-year-old"—then you're likely to ditch the process and just sit there and commiserate: "You're right. This really is a tough problem. Just let me tell you what my daughter did last week . . ." Your shift of Focus creates interference that obstructs your Faith ("I'm not sure this can be solved") and your Fire ("I'm not excited about trying to help you when I don't think I can even help myself"), and therefore impedes your performance. In other situations, coaches get emotionally caught up in the right/wrong mechanism. They get ego-invested and start judging, responding, defending, correcting, or explaining instead of simply moving on.

Again, one of the best ways to avoid this problem is to thoroughly plan ahead of time and, again, to keep the Goal clearly in mind. Another key is to remember that you have no need to explain, defend, or justify anything; only to clarify choices and consequences and help the person reach a point where he/she is willing to engage in a performer-driven conversation.

4. Falling into "+K" Coaching. Because most of us are in the habit of giving advice—and because we're in the midst of a cultural collusion that reinforces it—it's often hard to keep from falling back into outside-in (or "+K") coaching. It's hard to keep from just telling people what to do.

One way to avoid falling into this mistake is to watch the results of your coaching more carefully. Most people stop doing outside-in coaching only when they realize that it's not delivering what they think it delivers. Another way is to be rigorous in following the process. In other words, control what you pay attention to (what you Focus on) because that's what changes your Faith (your belief about what to do) and your Fire (your energy or passion about doing it).

5. Making Comfort the Driving Force. Despite centuries of historical evidence (and our own personal evidence) to the contrary, most of us seem to think that happiness and success come from the absence of challenge rather than in overcoming it. As a result, we try to avoid anything that creates immediate discomfort or pain. However, if we're really making a difference as coaches, much of the time—perhaps a majority of the time—we're not going to be comfortable.

Really getting into the world of a performer with a different thinking and/or decision-making style can be challenging. In addition, the very process of helping a performer discover (rather than telling him/her) what to do may create discomfort at first.

But we need to keep asking ourselves those three critical questions:

> What makes life difficult is that the process of confronting and solving problems is a painful one . . . Fearing the pain involved, almost all of us, to a greater or lesser degree, attempt to avoid problems . . . Yet it is in this whole process of meeting and solving problems that life has its meaning.
>
> M. SCOTT PECK,
> American psychiatrist and author

- Who is this about—the performer . . . or me?
- When I speak, whose need is getting met—the performer's or mine?
- Am I reducing interference . . . or increasing it?

If we are truly committed to making a difference in the lives of our performers, we can prioritize the end result over our temporary discomfort. We can learn to listen to others without taking ownership of their pain. We can keep reminding ourselves that the results that come from the uncomfortable, difficult conversations will often make the greatest difference in performance. Many of these things come naturally as we go through our own inside-out process before engaging in difficult conversations.

The Faith of the Coach

When you get down to it, all of these mistakes are a result of the Faith or belief of the coach. As we said earlier in this book, *belief drives behavior*. So if you don't *believe* planning is important or you *believe* that it's a bother and takes too much time, you're going to go into difficult conversations with little or no planning.

If you *believe* that you really know what's best for someone and that his/her performance will best be improved by simply listening to you and doing what you say, then you're not going to listen to that person or do the things that really engage his/her Faith, Fire, and Focus.

If you *believe* that what's comfortable for you or what's worked for you in the past is good enough or that your ad-libs are likely better than the questions anyway, you're not going to exercise the discipline to go through the GROW process in a way that will bring the highest performance results.

If you *believe* coaching should always be a pleasant experience or that you can be comfortable and still get results, you're not going to have the Fire to engage in the difficult conversations that will really make a difference in the life of your performer.

Above all, in coaching, if you don't *believe* in the power of the learner inside the performer—that curious, confident, wonderfully exploratory, child-like individual that's just waiting to be released—it will be all too easy to keep on judging (good/bad/right/wrong), to keep on trying to change people instead of making it safe for them to explore what they are and what they can do.

COACH'S PREPARATION CHECKLIST

Clarify your thinking (GROW yourself)

- ❏ Recognize your own issue.
- ❏ What will get the performer's attention?
- ❏ What will you do if you can't get the performer's attention?

Plan the conversation

- ❏ Keep the S.M.A.R.T. Goal for the conversation in mind.
- ❏ Identify language for each phase of the conversation.
- ❏ Anticipate the performer's possible responses.

Conduct the conversation

- ❏ Share your intentions—repeatedly.
- ❏ Identify language for each phase of the conversation.
- ❏ Demonstrate understanding.
- ❏ Ask for buy-in—repeatedly.

When you engage in inside-out coaching, you realize that your satisfaction does not come in *being seen* as a fountain of great wisdom; it comes in *seeing* the Faith, Fire, and Focus of the person you are coaching unfold. You realize that this is not about *you*; it's about *them*. It's about seeing the learner in them begin to emerge, to peek out, to test the waters, and to say, "Hey, I can do this!"

"I can do it." (Responsibility)
"I can do it." (Possibility)
"I can do it." (Actionability)

That kind of Faith releases Fire, energy, and excitement to perform. That Faith also directs Focus toward the critical variables that create results. And that Focus, in turn, increases Faith and Fire, creating an upward spiral of increasingly improved performance.

Reflective Questions

- Think of a difficult conversation you've recently had (or need to have) with someone.
  — What is it that made (or makes) this conversation difficult for you?
  — How did (or does) interference affect your Faith, Fire, and Focus as a coach?
  — What beliefs did (or do) you hold about this person?
  — What are the effects of these beliefs?
  — What beliefs would you like to hold?

- Who might be willing to engage with you in a role play of a difficult conversation:
  — At work?
  — At home?

Chapter 6: For an exercise that will help you
USE GROW TO PREPARE FOR A DIFFICULT COACHING CONVERSATION
Access the online community at
Alan-Fine.com

CHAPTER SEVEN

Inside-out in Teams and Organizations

Making good decisions and making them happen quickly are the hallmarks of high-performing organizations.

PAUL ROGERS AND MARCIA BLENKO,
partners in Bain & Company

n the early 1990s, I was doing training several times a year in a small niche of IBM as part of their consultant development program. When the company hit bottom in 1993—losing over $8 billion on $64 billion in revenue— I saw the culture become frantic. People were running around like chickens with their heads cut off. IBM had been held up as the epitome of what a good organization should look like. People had never felt insecure in their jobs before. The company had always hired smart people, and as long as those people remained competent, they'd had a job. But things had changed. Everyone was panicked that the company was going to fail, and nobody knew how to save it. There was a huge amount of negative energy, and it was essentially focused on "Isn't it awful?" "We're doomed." "Poor me. What do I do to survive?"

In April of that year, Louis Gerstner was hired to replace the former CEO, and things immediately began to change. The following year IBM earned $2.9 billion on $64.1 billion in sales[1], and the company continued to show strong results throughout Gerstner's nine-year tenure as CEO. The story is one of the most well documented turnarounds in business history.

As I've looked back on that situation through the lens of K3F (Knowledge, Faith, Fire, and Focus), I've come to realize that what Gerstner changed wasn't the *Knowledge* in the organization; what he changed was the *Focus*—what people were paying attention to. He shifted the Focus from bemoaning the situation and trying to figure out how to survive to immediate, doable action.

Giving people something immediately doable to Focus on eliminated a lot of the interference and changed their Faith, or belief. Instead of "This is hopeless," they began to say, "Oh, this is what I need to focus on next." That change in Faith created a change in energy, or Fire, and the company began to gain momentum. The momentum began to increase Faith even more, which released more Fire, more momentum, and more Faith, creating an upward spiral of improved performance and improved results.

Put simply, what happened to IBM on the organizational level is the same thing that happened to Jim on the tennis court. Creating Focus reduced interference and improved performance.

In this chapter, we're going to explore how the inside-out approach can help create breakthrough performance in teams and organizations. Although the focus of this chapter will be on business, the principles apply in all kinds of teams and organizations, including athletic teams, community organizations, musical groups, and even families—as you will see in chapter 8.

SayDoCo™: The Nuts and Bolts of a High-Performance Culture

One of the key differences in dealing with individual performance issues and team/organizational performance issues is in the level of complexity. With teams and organizations:

- You're trying to bring speed and accuracy to decision making that involves people and groups with nonaligned or competing, often disparate, needs.
- You're dealing with team and organizational "stories" as well as individual "stories" about why things are the way they are.
- You're dealing with the interpersonal dynamics of the team as well as the issues themselves.
- You have to consider external realities (such as the economy, the market, the competition, government regulations, and stakeholder feedback) as well as internal realities (such as organizational structure, policies, and cultural health).

For many people, the increased complexity itself creates huge interference. The way most managers and leaders attempt to deal with this complexity is through the outside-in (+K) approach. They pour huge amounts of time and money into training around "empowerment," "engagement," "trust," and "accountability" because they believe (and rightly so) that these four fundamentals will lead to better performance. But as we noted in chapter 1, of the billions of dollars spent annually on training and consulting, most is spent on information that is being repeated—and still not implemented—in organizations.

Being a simple Welshman, I always try to get things down to a nuts-and-bolts level. So as I think about these fundamental concepts, what shows up for me is that we all want to work with people who

- say what they'll do;
- do what they say; and
- communicate if they find they can't.

I call this "SayDoCo" for short. SayDoCo is the lifeblood of organizations. It's the key to Decision Velocity (speed and accuracy in decision making) and execution. It's how people interact together to get predictable, sustainable results. When people SayDoCo, empowerment, engagement, trust, and accountability naturally develop or increase. When they don't SayDoCo, these high-performance elements diminish or disappear.

When I work with groups, I often ask people whether they believe they personally SayDoCo, and almost everyone says yes. But when I ask the same group if they see their peers more than occasionally *not* SayDoCo-ing, again almost everyone says yes. The group is usually silent for a moment as they recognize the implication. Clearly, this is another of those places where there's a significant gap between what people think they do and what they actually do.

So what keeps people from SayDoCo-ing? The same thing that gets in the way of any other performance—interference. People are afraid to "say what they'll do" because they're worried that they won't be able to carry it out. They're afraid they might get distracted or derailed, or something might come up that would prevent them from accomplishing what they set out to do. They're fearful about what might happen if they disappoint their colleagues or their boss or the extra work that could be piled on them if they do deliver. As a result, they're hesitant to make a commitment. Or on the other hand, they may make a commitment they know they can't carry out just to please others in a meeting. They may misrepresent the realities or even lie to avoid or postpone confrontation or disappointment.

People don't "do what they say" because they do make unrealistic commitments or allow things to distract or derail them. Sometimes they become immobilized by fear—"I can't do this." "I'm not going to be able to meet the deadline." "What if my boss doesn't like my work?"—which blocks the Knowledge, Faith, Fire, and Focus they need to carry out the task.

People don't "communicate immediately if they find they can't" because they become distracted by concerns instead of focusing on the task. They worry that communicating the need to renegotiate could be perceived as an admission of failure, so they try to avoid it. Not wanting to become the scapegoat, many simply put their heads in the sand and hope everything will somehow work out in the end.

The net result of all this interference getting in the way of SayDoCo is that people don't trust each other. They begin to believe they can't depend on what others say, on the commitments they make, or on the ability of the group to work together or perform (Faith). Because of this belief, they're not excited about their job or fully engaged (Fire). What energy they do have is often directed in negative ways—cynicism, blaming, accusing, backbiting, and politicking. They pay more attention (Focus) to protecting their own interests and surviving until the weekend than they do to saying what they'll do, doing what they say, and communicating if they find they can't.

When leaders and mangers try to fix these problems (which they see as lack of empowerment, engagement, trust, and accountability) with the outside-in (+K) approach, their efforts often end up not only not solving the problems but also creating even more interference. An acquaintance of mine recently told me about his experience in the chemical industry:

> It seemed like every year they had a new initiative, a new strategy, new consultants or some new quick-fix opportunity, and it just kept wearing us down. Pretty soon, the company leaders lost all our attention. Annual strategy meetings just became another huge source of interference. They took us further away from our goal. I guess it was the unintended consequence of management's good intentions. They wanted to help us, but what they were doing was creating the exact opposite of the result they wanted.

With the inside-out approach, the focus is on developing a sustainable high-performance culture that *reduces* interference, thereby enabling people to consistently release Knowledge, Faith, Fire, and Focus and work creatively and synergistically together to accomplish shared goals. It's not just about getting immediate results; it's about creating the capacity to get those results consistently.

THE IMPACT OF SAYDOCO

The basic activities of SayDoCo are the building blocks of empowerment, engagement, accountability, and high trust—and therefore of a sustainable high-performance culture. For example, Gallup research shows that when people in an organization are engaged, the workplace is

- 50 percent more likely to have lower turnover;
- 56 percent more likely to have higher-than-average customer loyalty;
- 38 percent more likely to have above-average productivity; and
- 27 percent more likely to report higher profitability.[2]

A 2008 BlessingWhite study[3], however, shows that only 29 percent of North American workers are engaged, 19 percent are completely disengaged, and another 13 percent are disillusioned and at risk of becoming disengaged. A 2007 Towers Perrin Global Workforce Study puts the worldwide employee engagement figure at only 21 percent.[4]

By increasing SayDoCo, teams and organizations can increase engagement (as well as the other high-performance fundamentals), and the way to increase SayDoCo is through Focus.

For the most part, low empowerment, low engagement, low trust, and low accountability are symptoms of the deeper problem of failing to SayDoCo. The inside-out approach is more about eliminating the interference that's getting in the way of SayDoCo and creating the symptoms in the first place. The way we reduce interference in teams and organizations is the same way we reduce interference in coaching and individual performance—through focused attention. At the simplest level:

- The key to a high-performance culture is SayDoCo.
- The key to increasing SayDoCo is reducing interference.
- The key to reducing interference is Focus.
- The key to creating Focus is through GROW.

Team GROW

Fundamentally, organizations are made up of teams—including executive teams, sales teams, advertising teams, marketing teams, cross-functional teams, quality teams, and project teams. Let's take a look at how GROW might reduce interference in a typical team meeting.

Imagine it's 4:30 p.m. You're sitting in a meeting that was supposed to have been finished an hour ago. As someone makes a comment that will clearly create yet another delay, you sigh with frustration. You think, "These meetings always take too much time, and we hardly ever get anything done!" As you sit back in your chair wondering why, you reflect on all that's been going on. One member of the team has been doing most of the talking (as usual). Several other team members have been arguing back and forth over whose view of the problem—and/or the solution—is "right." One person has persisted in defending a solution she came up with before the data was even presented or there was any degree of clarity on the goal. Various team members who think differently (the man from Asia and the woman from Oklahoma; the person from engineering and the person from sales; the employee who's been in the organization for thirty years and the one who was hired last month) aren't communicating on the same wavelength. And one of the deeper thinkers—who often has some of the best solutions—is sitting stone-faced and silent at the end of the table with his arms folded across his chest.

Hidden agendas are clearly at play. One team member keeps coming up with solutions that would center-stage the role of his department. Another repeatedly makes comments obviously calculated to win the attention and approval of the team leader. One woman keeps looking at her watch and agreeing to comply with almost any solution that will get her out of the meeting. You can tell that in the end, her compliance will never carry the power of commitment.

The internal dialogue going on in people's heads is distracting. "So who called this meeting anyway?" "What's the agenda?" "Who's supposed to be in charge?" "Are any of these people as cynical as I am about this meeting?" "Even if we agree on a solution, will it actually be carried out?" "Are people really buying in?" "Where's the clarity on assignments and accountability?" "Are we going to be having this same meeting, trying to resolve the same problem, days, weeks, or months down the road?"

We've all been in meetings like this. And we've probably all been frustrated. But what we may not have had are the tools to help us understand what creates these kinds of situations and what we can do about it.

Like individuals, teams typically get to a decision by interacting around the four stages of GROW, but they, too, usually do it in a random (and not very effective) manner. Often there's no clear, shared vision of a S.M.A.R.T. Goal. Team members spend hours debating Reality and judging Options and never commit to an agreed-upon Way Forward. As a result, significant time, energy, and money are wasted—not only in the meeting but also in costly rework.

Whenever you're dealing with, say, five different team members' goals, five different Realities, five different perspectives on Options and opinions about the best Way Forward, things can get very confusing.

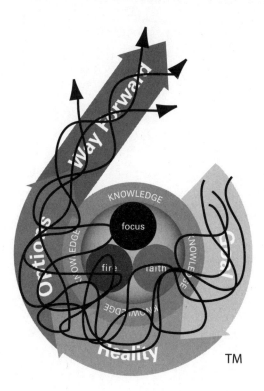

Giving the decision-making process common structure and language enables team members to interact more effectively and come to a viable Way Forward more quickly, significantly reducing interference, enhancing SayDoCo, and improving the performance of the team.

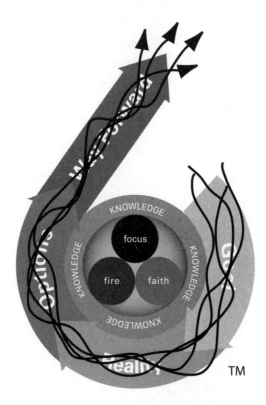

The following is an example of how simple Team GROW can be. In this situation, we're dealing with a small company's challenge to meet shipping needs more economically while still maintaining or even increasing customer satisfaction.

With an understanding of the basic steps of the process, the team sets up a whiteboard or large Post-it chart divided into four quadrants to keep track of input in each area. After deciding on someone to lead the discussion, team members focus on giving input concerning the **Goal** for the meeting—"Okay, what is it we want to get out of the next two hours? What do we want to walk away with?" Asking these questions encourages team members to

- focus on the purpose of the meeting (to the exclusion of the myriad of other distracting issues that could create interference);
- feel a shared commitment to problem-solving within the time frame;
- be realistic about what can be accomplished in the time frame; and
- work toward precision and accountability in the solution.

Someone captures all the ideas in the upper-right-hand quadrant on the chart, and team members agree on the one or two specific goals that would make the most critical performance difference. Whatever Goal is set for the meeting is a S.M.A.R.T. Goal. In the team scenario, that means it is Specific, Meaningful, *Agreed to*, Realistic, and Time-phased.

Once the Goal is agreed upon, each person shares his/her view of the **Reality** the team is facing. In this phase, *there is rarely a need for a consensus.* (This is where many typical team meetings get bogged down.) In fact, as long as there's an agreed-upon Goal, divergent realities actually bring more options to the table. So what's important here is that all team members get "air time" and that everyone has the benefit of the perspective of everyone else on the team.

The agreed-upon process and time frame encourage team members to be precise and succinct in presenting their points of view. In addition, this phase enables team members to

- gain a more holistic and accurate perspective of the issue;
- listen to others with confidence that their own opinion will be heard; and
- have confidence that the solution will include the thinking of everyone on the team—including the deep thinkers who are often the most quiet.

Realities are captured on the lower-right-hand quadrant of the chart.

With all the perspectives on the table, the team is ready to brainstorm **Options.** It is extremely important that evaluation and judgment are withheld until every idea is out so this phase can encourage creativity, out-of-the-box thinking, and "piggybacking" of ideas. Options are listed on the lower-left-hand quadrant of the chart.

Once the ideas are all out, the team moves toward a **Way Forward**. Ideas are evaluated. Options are narrowed down to those that seem most likely to create the desired results. From those, the team chooses a Way (or Ways) Forward that includes specific accountabilities with time frames. The Way Forward is written in the upper-left-hand quadrant of the chart.

The objective of what we could call "Team GROW" is to shift the Focus of the group from blaming and complaining about the disparity between where they are and where they want to be to focusing on something they think they can do (going through the stages of GROW). It's the shift from *why* it

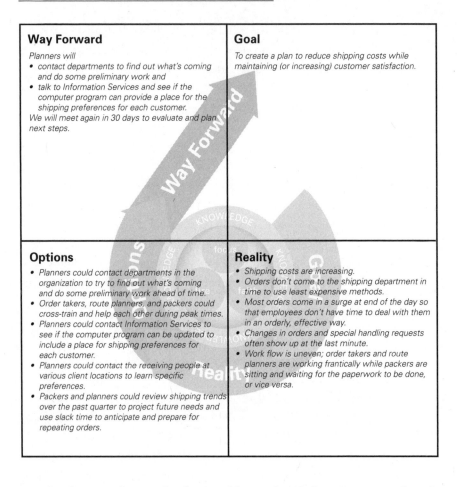

Way Forward

Planners will
- *contact departments to find out what's coming and do some preliminary work and*
- *talk to Information Services and see if the computer program can provide a place for the shipping preferences for each customer.*
We will meet again in 30 days to evaluate and plan next steps.

Goal

To create a plan to reduce shipping costs while maintaining (or increasing) customer satisfaction.

Options

- *Planners could contact departments in the organization to try to find out what's coming and do some preliminary work ahead of time.*
- *Order takers, route planners, and packers could cross-train and help each other during peak times.*
- *Planners could contact Information Services to see if the computer program can be updated to include a place for shipping preferences for each customer.*
- *Planners could contact the receiving people at various client locations to learn specific preferences.*
- *Packers and planners could review shipping trends over the past quarter to project future needs and use slack time to anticipate and prepare for repeating orders.*

Reality

- *Shipping costs are increasing.*
- *Orders don't come to the shipping department in time to use least expensive methods.*
- *Most orders come in a surge at end of the day so that employees don't have time to deal with them in an orderly, effective way.*
- *Changes in orders and special handling requests often show up at the last minute.*
- *Work flow is uneven; order takers and route planners are working frantically while packers are sitting and waiting for the paperwork to be done, or vice versa.*

can't be done to *what* can be done and *how*. That shift in Focus significantly reduces internal interference, including the interference created by the interaction of the group. It increases the ability of team members to SayDoCo because the shared Goal and everyone's Realities are clear, the Options represent the best thinking of all involved, and the Way Forward is S.M.A.R.T. and therefore easier to carry out. People are more focused on accomplishing the Goal than on their fears about whether or not they can do it. They're more interested in communicating for quick course correction if needed than in worrying about what other people might think.

As I've watched teams use GROW in a variety of situations over the years—particularly in business situations—it's become obvious to me that generally those who exercise the discipline to go through the GROW questions for teams carefully resolve their issues and come up with a viable Way Forward within the allotted time frame. And those who don't . . . don't. They get stuck. They run out of time.

GROW QUESTIONS FOR TEAMS

With slight variation, the specific questions in each of the four areas of GROW can be enormously helpful in using the process with teams.

Goal

What topic do we want to discuss?
What do we want from this discussion? (What's our S.M.A.R.T. Goal?)
What are the consequences if we do not reach this goal?

Reality

Briefly, what's been happening?
What have we tried so far?
What were the results?
What's our sense of the obstacles for us? For others (if others are involved)?
Is the goal still realistic?

Options

Describe fantasyland—if we could do anything, what might we do?
If others are involved, what would they need to see or hear to get their attention?
If we were watching this conversation, what would we recommend?
Do any of these ideas interest us enough to explore further?
If we were to do this, how might we go about it?

Way Forward

Does this option interest us enough to take action?
How will we go about it?
What might get in the way?
How might we overcome that?
What and when is the next step?

Generally, the best ways to avoid common mistakes for groups or teams are almost the same as those for individuals:

1. GOAL: Make sure it's S.M.A.R.T. (Specific, Meaningful, Agreed-to, Realistic, and Time-phased).
2. REALITY: Make sure it's accurate and complete. Keep in mind that *it's not necessary to reach consensus*—only to ensure that everyone feels confident that his/her reality is out on the table. Teams can easily get bogged down when members push for buy-in on their version of the problem.
3. OPTIONS: Make sure to really brainstorm.
4. WAY FORWARD: Again, make sure it's S.M.A.R.T.

Most often managers and team leaders can lead the process naturally as part of their role. However, as with the individuals, it's sometimes helpful for teams to get assistance from an independent facilitator or coach.

Facing a Hostile Group of Employees

Let me share an example of how Ken—the president of a small marketing company—used SayDoCo and GROW to turn his company around. For a number of years, Ken and Richard managed the company together. After a dispute arose between them, Ken suddenly found himself running the company on his own. He faced a hostile group of employees—partly because he had been naive and inexperienced in leadership and had behaved in some ways that created doubt and distrust in the past, but mostly because Richard had been blaming him "for everything that had gone wrong, including the weather." Richard had belittled Ken even to the point of telling him to not come into the office, insisting that no one liked his management style and no one wanted him there. When Ken asked for specifics, Richard's answers were vague and unsatisfying. Nevertheless, Ken stayed away from the office and worked at home for several months.

However, with Richard's departure, Ken suddenly needed to go back into the hostile environment that had rejected him. Ken was nervous. He was concerned that people would not respond to his leadership. In his words, "I had been their scapegoat for everything. I needed a plan, and I needed to understand my own failings and what had to happen to fix things with my employees. I needed people to be willing to give me and the company another chance."

In the midst of this challenging situation, Ken learned about SayDoCo and GROW and decided to use these tools on his first day back. Clearly, some key people were not happy he was there. One spoke no more than five words to him that first day, and another quit within two weeks. Nevertheless, Ken kept his Focus on saying what he'd do, doing what he said, and communicating if he found he couldn't. He held GROW meetings with each of the key people, who eventually opened up about their concerns. He used the inside-out tools to work through some very challenging situations. He ended up hiring a CFO and forming an executive team, which he took on a retreat to GROW their plans for the year. Six months later, Ken said:

> Everyone believes in this company again and is putting their best effort into it. As one previously disgruntled employee said, our company has undergone a complete transformation. It's as though these tools have given us super powers. People have been willing to give me, and more importantly, the company, a second chance. And with that opening, we have been able to make the most of it. I am able to lead.

By SayDoCo-ing himself and GROWing the company to create a culture of SayDoCo, Ken was able to create the empowerment, engagement, trust, and accountability that turned his company—and his own performance—around.

Bridging Personalities and Cultures

GROW can bring simplicity to the complexity of people working together in any kind of team or organization. This includes people of different ages, experience levels, personality types, and cultures, making it particularly relevant in today's cross-cultural world. While there may be *style* differences in various cultures and countries, I have yet to find any *stage* differences as far as decision making is concerned.

One manager in a large multinational company team said this about how her diverse team found a way to work together:

I have twelve people on my leadership team. It's very diverse. I am an American, and we have a Canadian, a Saudi Arabian, several Germans, a Brit, an Italian and an Austrian on the team. In the past, we tended to wallow in Reality. We really loved to talk about the details of our problems, but we were not able to move on to find Options to make a decision. So we started facilitating ourselves in these situations where we found ourselves becoming stuck. Now we stop, take out a flip chart, write the GROW model up on the flip chart and work from there. It really has helped us to move forward when we couldn't reach consensus to make a decision.

This manager also mentioned some important watch-outs in working with such a diverse team.

In any group situation, you have to be careful because the biggest personalities in the room or those who are the most competent in English can very easily drive a decision without having the rest of the group aligned. Those are the decisions that require a lot of re-work and a lot of follow-up and re-discussion afterwards.

However, when we really invest up front into reaching an aligned decision, I never have to follow up because the group is committed and the group goes and gets it done. That's where I think GROW really helps us, because it's either find a structured way to get everybody's input out on the table or spend time in follow-up meetings to rediscuss decisions.

I've also discovered that if an individual does not perceive that his/her reality has been acknowledged by the group, he/she will never move out of Reality. The whole group can be on Options and suddenly a person in the back of the room goes, "Well, I really think the problem is . . ." And the whole group says, "What in the heck are you talking about? That was Reality. We finished Reality forty-five minutes ago!" But clearly, the person didn't perceive that the rest of the team had acknowledged his/her perception of reality.

And part of it's cultural. On my team, the Americans and the Germans tend to say, "Been through Reality, you missed the boat, sorry, moving on." The more Mediterranean team members say, "Hey, we just weren't ready to talk about it. You can't ignore us because we don't process things in the same way you do."

So we found it was very important to get everyone's input out on the GROW chart. Metaphorically speaking, Joe says, "I think that orange has six bruises on it," and Peter says, "No, it only has one bruise on it," and Bernard says, "There are no bruises on it, it's a perfectly good orange, let's peel it and eat it." If we write all those perceptions down on the chart, then everyone can say, "Okay. Everybody knows how I see the situation, so we can move on."

As team members learn how to use GROW, they can transform their cultural, experiential, personality, or age differences from stumbling blocks to a rich seedbed of synergy, enabling them to increase Decision Velocity and create better, more broadly relevant and applicable high-performance solutions.

A Framework for Leadership/Management Tools

GROW can also provide an overarching framework for the various approaches in the tool kits managers and leaders carry. Rather than precluding these approaches, it gives them added value. (See chart on page 154.)

Many managers and leaders have told me that simply seeing how the things they're already doing fit in this framework gives them a whole new perspective. It helps them realize that what they're doing is part of one of the stages of decision making. They consider GROW as something of an orienteering tool that enables them to use these various approaches more effectively and keeps them from getting lost in one aspect of a particular phase.

After learning to use GROW, one technology company positioned the sales management approach they were using (Target Account Selling—or TAS) as a tool to better define their Reality. They felt that TAS enabled them to be more precise. Though this company had been using TAS before, they found that GROW created the lens through which TAS became even more powerful in meeting their needs.

Similarly, almost any program designed to improve team performance can be integrated with the GROW model. These targeted programs can often provide greater insight into a particular stage of GROW. The watch-out in using any program is to make sure it doesn't create interference instead of reduce it.

Creating Focus Throughout the Organization

As we've seen, creating Focus has a direct impact on performance. Every organization deals with performance issues on three levels: organizational, team,

How Other Tools Fit in the GROW™ Framework

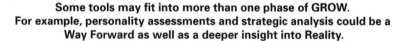

Way Forward	Goal
Project planning Strategic planning Action plans Tactical planning Time management Win-win agreements	Goal setting Goal cascading Mission Vision Values Strategic plans
Options	**Reality**
Brainstorming Idea generation Visioning Creating solutions Mind mapping	Balanced Scorecard SWOT analysis Force Field Analysis Team assessments Personality assessments Strategic analysis Organizational design analysis Leading and lagging indicators

**Some tools may fit into more than one phase of GROW.
For example, personality assessments and strategic analysis could be a
Way Forward as well as a deeper insight into Reality.**

and individual contributor. The ability to accelerate Decision Velocity on each of these levels is critical for companies in today's economy. In some cases, it can mean the difference between the survival and failure of an organization. At the very minimum, it provides a strong competitive advantage. By increasing Focus, GROW leads to increased Decision Velocity on all levels.

Creating Focus Throughout the Organization

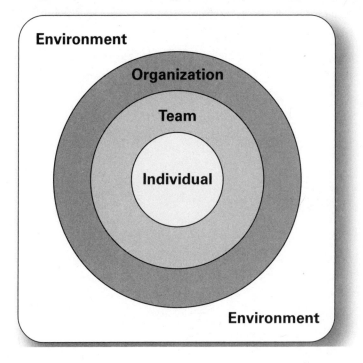

On the Organizational Level

CEOs and senior managers can use GROW in the following ways:

- To look outward at the environment and say, "What is it we're trying to achieve or contribute? What is our purpose for existing as an organization? What need out there are we going to try to reach?"
- To look at the financial, physical, ecological, and market Realities and explore the Options generated by those Realities. They can then choose the Way Forward—the organizational strategy—that makes the most sense. This repeatable process is particularly useful in today's world, where the environment is changing so rapidly that you can't just define organizational strategy once; you have to be constantly aware of what's going on and make adjustments or you can quickly become irrelevant.
- To look inward. "How do we operationalize our strategy?" "What do we need to do as an organization to accomplish our purpose or meet those

needs?" "Do our systems, structures, and policies focus attention on critical variables, or do they distract or cause interference?" "What Realities are we dealing with?" "Where are we now?" "What are our strengths?" "What strengths are we missing?" "Who do we have on board?" "What do we know?" "What don't we know?" Answers to questions such as these give birth to Options (expand research, partner with another group, realign a less-than-optimal system or policy, or invest in technology) and viable Ways Forward. The fact that the process is simple and repeatable makes it helpful in dealing with ongoing changes inside the organization.

On the Team Level

GROW takes effective decision making down to the marketing, advertising, customer service, and other teams created to make the Goals of the organization happen. Managers and team leaders can use GROW

- to identify the Goals and deal with the Realities, Options, and Ways Forward unique to their specific areas of responsibility;
- *with* their teams to address performance issues;
- *on* their teams to improve the way people work together; and
- to coach individual contributors on the team and to prepare for difficult conversations if needed.

On the Individual Level

With or without a coach, contributors can use GROW

- to align their efforts with the Goals of the organization and work toward improved performance in their particular role and
- to prepare for difficult conversations with colleagues or even with a boss.

The ultimate purpose of GROW is to increase Faith, Fire, and Focus and leverage Knowledge in the organization. On every level, focused attention can help people translate intent into action and promise into performance with accuracy and speed. It opens the door for people to deal with real issues, real concerns, and viable implementation strategies in their specific roles and situations.

GROWing performance issues has the added benefit of increasing SayDoCo. It focuses attention by providing a common process and language that enhance communication and execution throughout the organization.

The Organization with Faith, Fire, and Focus

Some of us have had the experience of being part of a team or an organization with high Faith, Fire, and Focus—whether in sports, business, the family, or some other situation. We've been so engaged and aligned with the vision, mission, and culture, the overwhelming feeling is, "I want to be here! I've got to be a

> You cannot have an execution culture without robust dialogue— one that brings reality to the surface through openness, candor, and informality.
>
> LARRY BOSSIDY, former chairman of Honeywell International, and RAM CHARAN, business consultant, speaker, and writer

part of this!" Some of us have had the exact opposite experience, where we find ourselves consistently counting the minutes until we can go home and go do something meaningful or enjoyable. Even in observing, it's easy to tell the difference between teams and organizations in which Faith, Fire, and Focus are high and those in which they are low.

An organization *with* Faith has a clear, compelling sense of mission and purpose that is effectively communicated to and passionately believed in by people on every level of the organization. People have a strong "We can!" belief and a firm conviction in the organization's resilience and ability to effectively learn and adapt in a changing environment. An organization *without* Faith is filled with fear, doubt, or lack of clarity concerning its value proposition as well as the value of the organization's purpose and/or its viability in changing circumstances.

An organization *with* Fire has a positive energy directed toward the accomplishment of the purpose of the organization. An organization *without* Fire is filled with apathy, lack of interest, and resigned compliance (rather than enthused commitment). What energy exists is often turned into negative fire, which is manifest in politicking, backbiting, and criticizing.

An organization *with* Focus has clearly articulated key priorities that lead to the accomplishment of the organization's purpose, and those priorities are given robust attention on every level. An organization *without* Focus is filled with distraction, miscommunication, redundant effort, waste of resources, and poor execution.

THE ORGANIZATION WITH AND WITHOUT FAITH, FIRE, AND FOCUS		
	With	**Without**
Faith	A clear, compelling sense of mission and purpose that is passionately believed in at every level A strong "We can!" belief in the organization's resilience	Fear, doubt, and/or lack of clarity about the organization's purpose and its viability in changing circumstances
Fire	A positive energy directed toward the accomplishment of the purpose of the organization	Apathy, lack of interest, and resigned compliance Negative energy manifested in politicking, backbiting, and criticizing
Focus	Clarity on key priorities and critical variables Constant attention to these priorities and variables on every level	Distraction, miscommunication, inconsistency, and/or redundant effort

Just as the inside-out approach can help a coach look at the individual performer in terms of Faith, Fire, and Focus as well as Knowledge, it can help managers and leaders look at teams and organizations through the same lens. And when teams and organizations move ahead with all four elements of high performance, the possibilities for breakthrough performance are truly amazing.

Reflective Questions

- Think of an experience you're having in working with a team or organization. What kinds of interference do you see created by the complexity of working with others? How is this interference affecting the level of your own performance and/or the performance of the group?

- What's it like when the people you work with SayDoCo (say what they'll do, do what they say, and communicate immediately if they can't)? What's it like when they don't? What's the impact on the ability of you and your group to perform?

- What do you notice about yourself when you SayDoCo well? When you don't do it well, what's getting in the way?

- How would you evaluate the level of Knowledge, Faith, Fire, and Focus in your team or organization? What kind of impact do you think this is having on performance? What do you think the team or organization could focus on to improve performance?

Chapter 7: For an exercise that will help you

EVALUATE YOUR TEAM'S FAITH, FIRE, AND FOCUS AND USE GROW TO IMPROVE PERFORMANCE

Access the online community at

Alan-Fine.com

Part 3

PRACTICE

CHAPTER EIGHT

"How Do I Use This? Let Me Count the Ways . . ."

(With Apologies to Elizabeth Barrett Browning)

> The habit of the active utilization of well-understood principles is the final possession of wisdom.
>
> **ALFRED NORTH WHITEHEAD,**
> English philosopher and mathematician

One of the great pleasures I've enjoyed in working with the inside-out approach over the years has been hearing about the wide variety of creative ways in which people have used it as individuals, in coaching, and in their organizations and teams.

In this chapter I'd like to share a few of their stories in the spirit of creating more possibilities for you to consider. As you read each story, ask yourself, "What evidence do I see that Faith, Fire, and Focus are being released? What is it that created that release? And what is the impact on performance?" Taken all together, these stories reinforce the idea that inside-out is more than a process; it's a way of thinking and interacting with others that helps eliminate interference, increase Decision Velocity, and improve performance in any area of life.

The Fifteen-Minute Solution: Empowering an Employee

One day while I was driving to a nearby city, I received a call from one of my staff—a woman who has traditionally been a chronic complainer and very negative. She was calling to inform me of an issue she was having with one of her internal customers who did not understand our company process. In the past, I have addressed complaints from her by telling her steps to take. However, this time I decided to change my approach. As I was close to my destination when she called, I said, "We have fifteen minutes—what do you want to get out of it?" She was able to determine a S.M.A.R.T. Goal fairly quickly. Also, the set time helped me move her rapidly through the Reality stage and into fantasyland. We identified several Options, set up an action plan, and put a timeline on those actions.

The next day she reported the very successful results of the action plan and was happy to say, "Problem solved!" Not only was her issue solved and she was happy, but she thanked me for taking the time to help her solve her own problem. I firmly believe that with a few more of these sessions, she will be on the way to being able to do this herself.

Even a Young Performer Understands Interference

A few years ago, I was trying to help my eight-year-old son learn his multiplication tables. I'd been trying to make a game out of it because he was very competitive, so I'd said, "Let's practice with the flash cards, and then we'll time you and we'll track your improvement over time." We did that, and we had some success—though not as much as I would have expected.

After learning about the inside-out approach at work, I went home one night and decided to try it with my son. So I sat down with him and said, "Okay. What's the Goal here? What are we trying to do?" We talked about it, and then we talked about how we were trying to do it. And my son said, "Mom, all I'm thinking about is that timer. It's distracting me. If you want to tell me how I did after the test, that's fine. But can we get rid of the timer so I don't have to see it while I'm doing it?" So I said, "Okay, we'll try this." And we did, and of course, he did much better. As it turned out, what I'd thought was providing incentive had actually been creating interference instead.

I've learned that as both a parent and a manager, I tend to provide solutions. That's what I've been rewarded for my whole career. But GROW forces me to step back—to quit providing the solutions that would have worked for me, and instead think about the solutions that would work for other people. In some situations, it's more time consuming to walk through the process, but you definitely get a better result in the end.

Team GROW on the Baseball Field

A few years after I learned about the inside-out approach, my husband became the assistant coach for our fourteen-year-old son's baseball team. In the middle of one out-of-town tournament, the boys were really doing poorly, so the head coach called them together and said, "Okay boys, I want you to think about what your goals are, write them on a piece of paper, and put them under your pillow." When my husband came back and told me about it, I thought, "That's great, but how is that going to translate into improved performance?" Nevertheless, I didn't say anything. The boys went on to play with disastrous results.

After the tournament, I approached my husband and said, "Hey, I'd really like to teach the coaches some things I learned about performance at work. Would you have an objection if I inserted myself into this situation?" He said, "You know, I think it would actually be a good idea. We certainly need something!" So I approached the head coach, explained a little about removing interference, and offered to teach the coaching staff what I'd learned about dealing with it. He said, "Well, clearly we don't have the answers," and he acknowledged that he was willing to try something new. He even said, "You know, maybe the boys actually need to hear from somebody else. Why don't you teach it to them first? Then you can circle back around and teach us coaches."

A tournament had been scheduled for the following weekend, so I actually rented a spot in our local community sports center and brought in markers and flip charts and took the boys through the process. We began with Goals. Their first goal was, "We want to play better as a team." I said, "Okay, let's break it down. How do we play better as a team?" They decided that better team performance would be a result of better individual performance, so they set a team goal for each of them to meet with me so that I could help them set their individual goals.

Then we talked about Reality. They said they were playing poorly. They weren't playing as a team. They were getting frustrated. As they talked, it also came out that the coaches were actually creating interference. The head coach particularly tended to yell and scream at the boys. Evidently he thought this approach would motivate them, but it was having the opposite effect. They were afraid to try harder for fear of being yelled at if they did something wrong.

We talked about Options. They said they could stop playing in tournaments. They could get new team members. They could figure out a way to let the coaches know how their yelling was affecting them. They could just let the best players play. They could practice harder. I pointed out to them that simply trying harder doesn't necessarily translate into better performance if you don't have a goal. That led them to add another team goal: to place first in the upcoming tournament.

One of the options we finally decided on as our Way Forward was to have the GROW meetings with the individual players. In those meetings, my son, who was the catcher, said he wanted to throw six people out on base during the tournament. Another boy wanted to catch 90 percent of the fly balls that came his way. Another wanted to make sure he got on base every time he was up. They were simple goals, really, but they provided a clear Focus for each player.

Once the boys had all set their goals, I had them present the goals to their teammates. We made it fun with the markers and flip charts. Then we went to the coaches and the boys presented their individual and team goals to them. Afterward, I took the coaches aside and explained what we had done. As per my agreement with the boys, I also explained the problem with the interference they created by yelling and screaming.

That weekend when we went to the tournament, every one of the boys exceeded his goal in the very first game. So we set new goals for each of the other games and for the tournament as a whole. The boys ended up coming out in second place. They were so excited! And so were the coaches and parents.

The next season, I was asked to join the coaching staff. I was not a star athlete (nor had I ever been), and I'd never done any athletic coaching before, but the process was simple and it worked. Really, it was just about removing interference and getting the boys' focused attention.

Before this experience, I'd had success with the GROW process in my professional role, but I honestly had no idea that we would see that kind of performance improvement in the boys. And what was really exciting was to see the self-esteem and self-confidence they gained as a result. My son, who is now seventeen, still uses the process and still sets S.M.A.R.T. Goals.

"Focus on the End of the Beam!"

When I picked my daughter up from gymnastics practice on the evening after I attended GROW training, I could tell she was a little down. She's a level five competitive gymnast, and she had been struggling to make her cartwheel on the balance beam all season. She had finally reached the point where she was able to make some during practice, but she could never make one during a gymnastics meet. As we drove home, she kept talking about how frustrating this was and how she really wanted to make the cartwheel on the beam at the state meet on Saturday.

I thought this might be a good opportunity to use some of the training I had just received, so I started asking her questions to help get her focus off of the cartwheel itself. I asked if anything felt different when she did a good cartwheel versus when she fell off. I asked if there were any specific steps within the cartwheel itself that she could focus on. I told her that if she could avoid focusing on making the cartwheel on the beam and aim her focus else-where, it might help.

Though she couldn't think of anything in the car, when we arrived home she wanted to try some cartwheels on the beam with me watching. She tried several and fell off the majority of the time. I asked if there was a particular part of the beam that she could look at as she was doing the cartwheel. This question made her remember something her coaches had suggested earlier— to focus on the end of the beam as she was coming out of her cartwheel. I suggested she try some with this focus.

It was amazing. She made several cartwheels on the beam in a row. She was so excited. After she had made ten or more, she decided to try one without focusing on the end of the beam. She fell off again. She went back to focusing on the end of the beam and made several more. She was now ready to go to bed because she had solved her problem, and I could see that her confidence was back.

When I picked her up from gymnastics on Friday, she was very excited because she had kept her focus and had a very successful beam practice. Before she went out on the floor at Saturday's meet, I said two things to her: "Have fun" and "Focus on the end of the beam!" When the time came for her beam exercises, she made the cartwheel. At the end of her routine, she looked up in the stands and gave us the biggest smile I ever saw. Whatever else happened at that meet was irrelevant to her. She had finally met her goal on the beam, and that was all that mattered.

Helping a Two-year-old Find the "Paci"

My wife and I have two-year-old twin girls, Brooke and Breanna, who don't sleep well (which is probably because of my example in staying up late working on the computer). Tonight, Brooke came to me whining and asking for her pacifier. This would normally have been frustrating to me, as I was trying to get work done and she was still awake and in need of assistance/attention.

My typical response would have been to either go and get it for her as quickly (and begrudgingly) as possible or to yell at my wife in a frustrated and disturbed tone to get it, and then, clearly irritated, order Brooke back to bed. But tonight something about the inside-out approach clicked, and the conversation went something like this:

Me: "What's the matter, baby? What do you want?"

Brooke: "My paci [pacifier]." [*Bingo!—her Goal*]

Me: "Okay, honey. Where is your paci?"

Brooke: "Don't know. Can't find it anywhere." [*Simple Reality defined*]

Me: "Would you like to try and look harder for it if I help you look?" [*I led her into the Option of finding it on her own with perceived help.*]

Brooke: "Yeah." [*Bingo again! Commitment on her part to reach her Goal without complete dependence.*]

Me: "If I help you find it, will you go lie down for me?" (*throwing in my selfish Goal and leading her into a shared Way Forward beyond just finding the paci*]

Brooke: "Yeah!" [*her commitment to my Goal as well as hers and to our Way Forward*]

I went through the motions of looking around, but basically walked her through the process for herself. She soon found her pacifier under some bedding and was ecstatic that she had been able to find it on her own. After I sang her praises, she happily went to lie down in her bed as agreed. But then came an unexpected benefit. Her sister Breanna perked up, looked around, spotted her paci, ran and got it, and said, "Look, Daddy, I found my paci all by myself, too!"

I know this may sound trivial to some, but I imagine that anyone who's had experience with children can understand how monumental this was for us.

From Critics to Contributors at Work

One of my most memorable group coaching experiences was during my first year of using the inside-out process. We were making attempts to change our corporate culture to one that was more team-based. Our training team was tasked with delivering a number of new team-training courses to management and shop floor employees.

As I was delivering this training to one unit, I was constantly getting negative input and criticism from a few members. "This won't work." "Our management won't buy into this." "Every time we have a suggestion management blows it away." These were some of the comments they repeatedly gave during the training. I realized this was an opportunity for me to utilize the inside-out approach because without the buy-in from these critics, there really was very little chance for the unit to become more team-based.

I approached the management of the unit to ask for their permission to meet separately for two hours with the six members of the unit who were the most outspoken regarding the team training they had received. Management agreed and a meeting date and time was established.

In preparation for the meeting, I wrote each of the GROW questions on a separate sheet of flip-chart paper. Then as we began, I explained the purpose of the meeting: I wanted to better understand what barriers they were facing and why they felt the way they did. And if possible, I wanted to work with them to identify a plan of action to improve the chances of their becoming a highly productive team-based unit.

I then moved to the flip charts and we identified a S.M.A.R.T. Goal. This was no easy task, as these people were adamant that their unit could not become team-based under their current management. They were looking outside-in, not inside-out. Ultimately, we did arrive at a goal: to develop a plan of action by which we could work with our management to begin to improve the unit's teaming performance.

From that point on, I used each flip-chart question to keep them focused on the Realities, Options, and the Way Forward. As you recall, these were the most outspoken members of the unit, the ones who claimed, "This will never work." What came out of the meeting, however, was that their frustration was based on the fact that they fully endorsed teaming and wanted it to work! They were just too caught up in the blaming of management to see how they could make it happen.

After considerable discussion and ensuring that everyone had his/her Realities and Options identified and listed on the flip charts, we identified the option(s) they felt held the greatest potential for achieving success. The Way Forward they chose was to ask management to shut down the plant for a day in order to bring all three shifts together at the same time to discuss how to improve the lines of communication between management and the shop floor.

At first they felt that this would never happen. Management would never shut down the plant for something like this. And guess who they wanted to present this idea to management? That's right—me. I told them I would, but I also said I felt it would be far better if they presented the proposal themselves and walked them through the process we had just used to show their management how they arrived at this option. Two members of the group then agreed to approach their management with the plan. I am happy to report that their management agreed to the plant shutdown, and they held a very productive meeting that cleared the air and helped them take a significant, positive step in the teaming process.

I won't begin to state that everything was rosy from that time on for this unit, or that they turned into a highly productive team overnight. But this unit did move forward in their teaming efforts, and when we held additional team-training sessions, the individuals who were so defiant initially later became key contributors to the training discussions.

A Difficult Decision for a Widow at Eighty-one

I am an eighty-one-year-old widow. Recently the car I'd driven for ten years started having problems. When I took it in for an estimate, I was told it would cost $4,700 to repair. I was ready to pay to have it fixed, but the man at the repair shop said, "You know, even if you get the car fixed now, you will still have parts that are ten years old and could go out at any time. You might want to think about getting a new car."

Well, I didn't want to think about it. I loved my car. Before he died, my husband had gone to great lengths to find just the right car to meet my needs. It was a nice light color, it was easy to drive, and it had a hatchback so that I didn't have to bend down and pick things up out of a trunk with my bad back.

My emotional attachment to the car, plus the difficulty of making such a major spending decision with so many options and without the benefit of my husband's input, made the task seem overwhelming. I thought it would take me months to wade through all the possibilities and figure out what to do.

Then my daughter, who had learned about GROW, came over to my house and suggested that we go through the process. She began by saying, "Okay, what's your Goal?" I replied that it was to have safe, economical transportation. Then she said, "What are the Realities we're dealing with?" As we talked, we started to list them:

1. I was emotionally attached to my old car, but putting $4,700 into a ten-year-old car really didn't seem wise.
2. I needed dependable transportation. In addition to handling my personal needs, I was spending forty hours a week as volunteer director of our local literacy center, and I had to be able to get where I needed to go and sometimes haul supplies.

My daughter said, "So what's important to you in a car?" She helped me develop a list of priorities, which included things such as low cost, high safety and performance ratings, convenient rear loading, and four-wheel or all-wheel drive to handle our snowy winter roads. I added that not having to drive far to have the car serviced was really important to me, and my daughter pointed out that this priority immediately narrowed my choices down to cars sold by the two dealerships in our community.

So we began to look at Options. My grandson got some comparative information about various cars off the Internet. My daughter and I evaluated the possible options against my priority list, and we came up with the car that appeared to best meet my needs. When we went to the dealership, my choice was quickly confirmed.

It was still hard for me to say good-bye to my old car the following day, but after only a few tears I was able to drive away feeling really good about my decision. And I was amazed to realize that the process I thought would take months had taken only three days.

But there's another chapter to this story. About a week after I bought my new car, a friend told me about a car she had bought and how wonderful it was. I began to have doubts. I told my daughter I wished I had known about my friend's car before making my decision. My daughter immediately took me back to Reality. She said, "When we discussed the issues, you told me that one of your most important priorities was close service. Isn't that right?" I agreed that it was. "Has that priority changed?" I said it had not. "Well," she said, "if you had bought this other car, you'd have to drive twenty miles to get it serviced. So even if you had known about it, would it really have made a difference in your decision?"

I immediately realized it wouldn't. I'd identified my priorities, I'd made my choice based on those priorities, and those priorities hadn't changed. I was quickly brought back to feeling great about the decision I'd made.

"I'm Not Taking Any More Monkeys!"

When I came back from InsideOut training I promised myself, "I am through telling people what to do!" It just didn't work. Fifty percent of the time I was a genius and fifty percent of the time I was an idiot. So I said, "I'm not taking any more monkeys. I am not going to take on other people's actions or solve their problems for them."

So when I got a call from a woman in marketing who was having a tough time with her boss and wanted to get some ideas on how to best deal with her, I told her I'd be happy to meet with her. I asked her to set aside an hour and told her that I would be asking her some questions to help her get to a resolution.

When I got to the meeting, there were actually three people from the department waiting for me. They were all having trouble with this boss. So I started into the GROW process, and after the third or fourth question in the Reality phase, they stopped me and said, "Wait a minute! What's with all the questions?" I said, "I'm helping you gain perspective and create some context so that whatever solution you come up with will accomplish the results you want." They said, "We didn't ask you to come here and ask us all these questions. We want you to tell us what to do." I replied, "Well, I certainly could do that, but I don't think that's going to facilitate the best outcome. After this conversation, I get to go back to my desk, but you're the ones who have to go back and work with this individual. You know what's going on better than I do. My sense is that you can come up with a better solution than I ever will. I'll be happy to give you some ideas, but I'm not going to tell you what to do." Then I said, "Look, just humor me. Let's finish out this process and see what kind of result comes out of our conversation. Then we can go from there."

Finally they said, "Okay, fine. What's the next question?"

In the end, they came up with a solution that was much better than anything I could have come up with. And it was their solution. They owned it, and they had a lot of energy behind it.

Keeping a Talented Chef

Several years ago, I was working as HR director in a hotel environment. One day I was surprised to see two security officers escorting one of our talented culinary people into my office. Evidently there had been a huge blowup in the kitchen. This man had become enraged and had started screaming, and people had become so scared that they called in security, who had actually taken his knives away. Culinary people typically carry their own expensive knives with them in their aprons as part of their tools, and although this man was not creating an immediate threat, the officers were concerned because the conflict level was so high, so they asked him to hand over his knives.

When I began talking with this man, it became evident to me that he was deeply distressed. So I excused the security officers, who were very disconcerted. They thought this man was on the verge of violence and wanted to stay with me. But I had decided that I wasn't afraid of him, and I wanted to talk privately with him about what was going on.

I asked him to sit down, and I took him through the coach-driven GROW model. As he began to share his Reality, he became very open with me. I discovered that he was having intense difficulties in some personal relationships, and they were creating interference that was spilling out into all his relationships to the point that he was in jeopardy of losing his job. We looked at Options, which included continuing to try to ignore his problems, talking things over with his family or friends, or getting counseling help through the employee's assistance program. In the end, he decided to get counseling.

A short time later, I received a note from this man saying that our conversation had really helped him. In addition, the executive chef came to me and said, "I don't know what you did, but [this person] has had a complete turnaround since he's talked with you. We don't have a problem anymore." Later, he also sent me a note to thank me for being willing to have a conversation with this talented, but troubled, chef and help him resolve his problem.

Better Options, Better Relationship with a Teen

The other evening, my fourteen year-old daughter came to get my signature on a sheet of paper that would enable her to drop freshman band and move into a "seminar" class during the same hour. As she had played the flute since the fourth grade and had just made first chair in the freshman band, you can imagine the concern my wife and I had about her giving up that part of her life. She said she was having trouble with her mathematics course, and her guidance counselor (whom we later discovered had not really taken time to get the whole picture) had recommended a new tutoring program that would be held during school hours.

I sat down with her and started asking questions, as I usually would. However, after about the second question, it dawned on me that this would be an opportunity to apply the inside-out approach. So I regrouped and began to focus on what it was that she was trying to achieve (her Goal). We then reviewed the Realities of what she was struggling against (time, sports, math, time, church activities, singing at some of the school games—did I mention time?). While I tried to keep it brief, it was nearly impossible, given what she was facing. It was too easy to focus on what was not working, rather than on what was working.

When I felt that we'd painted a clear picture of what she was facing, I proceeded to ask her to think of Options—not only the ones she'd already considered, but others, regardless of what she might think were limitations. While most of the options she suggested were not surprising, they demonstrated to me that she was applying the mental effort needed for this stage. I was careful to not interject—just to keep listening and asking, "What else?" Finally, I asked her permission to offer a couple of suggestions.

Then we began to look for a Way Forward. While we were not able to immediately come up with a concrete plan, we did set in place a couple of possibilities for her to follow up on. When I asked for her buy-in, she gave it with none of the fussing that normally would have occurred.

As of today, she has followed up on one of the alternatives, and I've been able to meet with her counselor about the situation. It turns out that there were other alternatives that hadn't been considered because of the incomplete picture that was given to her. It looks like we may be able to salvage her academic efforts, while still allowing her to stay in the band. But even if she has to drop that class to accommodate a new schedule, she will still be able to get into a math class better suited to her needs.

More importantly, because of the additional time and effort I took with my daughter by using this approach and because of the methodical thought process it provided, she is more open to me than she has been for some time.

Anorexia: From Complications to Solutions

A little over a year ago, my sixteen-year-old daughter was diagnosed with anorexia. She got down to eighty-six pounds, and her extreme weight loss led to the development of a pulmonary lesion. After trying several different approaches unsuccessfully, we finally discovered a family-based treatment that brought results. Within a short time, her weight came up and she was starting to think properly—which was a huge achievement.

But she had two problems that were not getting resolved. One was that she was periodically "bingeing" (eating an excessive amount of food, which is often typical for anorexics in recovery), and that was causing her great distress. The second was that she was fanatically focused on the number 111. We had told her that if she went below 110, we would up the meal plan and down the exercise. And in her mind, she never wanted to be above 115. So it was, "111 . . . 111 . . . 111!" That focus was not proving helpful, but she couldn't seem to think of anything else.

When I offered to take this daughter through the GROW process to help her resolve these issues, she willingly agreed. We sat down together on the back porch. I handed her a copy of the GROW questions and she did the actual writing as we went through each one.

As we talked about her Goal, she began to realize that the issue wasn't about a number on the scale. What she really wanted was to be strong, muscular, toned, and energetic. She wanted to have endurance. When I asked her about the consequence of not reaching her goal, she said that she wouldn't feel happy. She wouldn't feel good about herself or the way she looked.

When we talked about Reality, she acknowledged that she had made excellent progress and was doing some good things—running, swimming, eating healthy meals and snacks—but said that her binges made her feel terrible. When I asked what had worked the best for her so far, she said walking away and doing something that distracted her from thinking about food, such as deep breathing or going for a walk. But sometimes it worked, and sometimes it didn't. When I asked about her sense of the obstacles she faced, she said that sometimes she would begin to feel anxious or even angry and out of control, but she couldn't pinpoint what stimulated those feelings. That would frighten her, and she would start thinking irrationally.

Before asking her if she thought her goal was still realistic, I assured her that we all have times when we feel anxious or angry or out of control. I said, "Realistically, you're not always going to feel strong, toned, and energetic, and you're not always going to do what you think is right in terms of eating and exercising. But do you still believe the goal is realistic? Do you think you could do this, say, eighty percent of the time?" After thinking about it, she said she felt it was. So she adjusted her goal. (For a perfectionist used to getting a 4.0-plus grade point average in school, this was a huge breakthrough, and it ended up making a big difference in her level of anxiety and her ability to handle the challenge.)

We talked about a number of Options. Her father and I could plan out her meals and snacks. She could always eat with someone else. She could eat more slowly. She could create a list of activities she could do that would distract her from worry about food, weight, and anxiety—things such as drawing, spending time with her pets, taking a walk, or doing activities on the computer.

In evaluating her options, she eliminated some because they took away her sense of control and independence. She eliminated others because with work and school schedules, they were not realistic.

The Way Forward she decided on involved the following steps:

1. Setting out healthy portions of the right foods for a meal in advance
2. Rationally recognizing that she's had enough after eating the right portions, taking note of how she feels, and then moving on to the next activity
3. Calling me immediately when she gets that "out-of-control" feeling
4. Asking her sister to help by not focusing on the irrational behaviors or comparing them with what she might do, but instead helping distract her by playing video or computer games with her or going outside to shoot hoops or practice volleyball

My daughter has now started her senior year at high school and is in a much different place now than she was last year. First and most importantly, she is healthy. She hasn't gone below 110. She is more social and outgoing. She has a job at a local theater. She still has times when she thinks she's fat and needs to lose, but those times are far less frequent and more normal for a teenage girl. She's looking forward to college, and I'm hopeful it will never get to the point where she will starve herself again.

I think one of the most important things GROW did was to take the Focus off the wrong thing—the obsession with the 111 pounds—and put it on how she wanted to feel. The number 111 was not an inspiring goal. It didn't capture her Fire, and going above 111 had a significantly negative impact on her Faith. But now she's excited about wanting to feel toned and energetic. She recently said, "Mom, the last time I did the run at school, it took me eight minutes. Now it's taking me three minutes, and I'm not even out of breath. I feel really, really good about doing it." Later, she said, "You know, I really don't care how much I weigh. Even if I'm 140, if I feel like I have strength and endurance and I look good in my clothes, I'm okay."

Looking back, I believe we could not have used GROW successfully when she was so ill. She had to get to a place where her body was being nourished and she was able to think straight first. But once that happened, we were able to use the GROW questions to really drill down on the problem and to chunk down the actions she could take to help her through her difficult moments.

Dealing with Alzheimer's

Several years ago, my mother was diagnosed with Alzheimer's. We have a large family—some in state, some out of state—and, of course, everyone was concerned about how we were going to deal with this. One brother in particular was not at all on board with the diagnosis or with the idea of using some of the prescribed medicines. So we decided to get everyone to come together for a family meeting to talk over what we wanted for our parents and how we would use our combined desires and resources to support them.

To make sure we were all in agreement on the goal, covered all the issues, and all had a chance to share (as some were prone to talk more than others), we decided to work with a facilitator. I came up with an agenda that I sent to everyone in advance. Though I didn't label it as such, the agenda basically went through the four steps of the GROW process. And although the facilitator was not familiar with it, he thought it was a good approach and was glad to use it.

We started out by coming to agreement about the Goal, which was to make sure that we were doing everything we could to allow our parents to stay together in their home as long as possible. There was clear agreement from everyone on that.

Then we started looking at the Realities. We acknowledged that—assuming Mom did have Alzheimer's—it was a progressive disease, and although we weren't going to be able to foresee what we would need to deal with later on, we could at least identify immediate action steps now and possible action steps for the future. We recognized that there was a disparity in income among the children—some family members could put much more into financial support, but couldn't be as present. We realized we had a lot of questions: Where could we find in-home help? Was it likely we could get anyone we could trust? Who could pay for it? How would we handle medications? How could we make her comfortable without sedating her? What other resources might be available when the home was no longer adequate?

When we got to Options, we listed everything for caregiving, from having some magical angel come and live with our parents 24/7 for free to more realistic alternatives, such as having our single widowed sister come and stay with them, moving them into a duplex owned by one brother and close to another, taking turns being with them a week at a time, me retiring early and staying with them full-time, patching together some kind of plan that had multiple people coming in, or scheduling grandkids to take turns helping out. We talked about options in other areas, including getting medical directives and powers of attorney in place, signing our parents up for meals-on-wheels, putting handrails in strategic places in the home, getting some housekeeping support, and visiting next-step care facilities so that we would be ready should the need arise.

In the end, since there were enough of us to carry out multiple options, our Way Forward included a number of those plus others. We did the handrails, the documents, the housekeeping support, and the meals-on-wheels. Some of us made commitments to read and share books about Alzheimer's. We encouraged Dad to sign up for a series of caregiver classes—not only to get him out of the house, but also to educate him concerning how he might take care of himself during this time. We investigated future care facilities, and we were all relieved when one family member said, "Look, Mom and Dad don't need to get long-term-care insurance. When the time comes, I'm ready. Just tell me how much is needed."

As I look back over the ensuing years—years filled with additional challenges, decisions, personal communications, e-mail communications, and Mom's eventual death—I realize that in addition to helping us create an effective action plan, two really important things came out of that initial meeting.

First, we agreed that we would trust each other, that we would not check up on each other or judge each other for what we could or couldn't do; we would assume that we were each doing our very best. In retrospect, maybe we should have taken things one step further along those lines, but overall that agreement created an environment of trust in which we were able to communicate and make decisions comfortably as things continued to change.

Second, the process we used in that meeting created a strong foundation for what transpired over the following years. As the disease progressed, we had significant challenges, particularly with the brother who really saw things differently. But because of that meeting, we had a Goal that we all understood and owned. And that goal took precedence over the disagreements. It got us to a place where in the end we could still come together and say good-bye to her and not let that difference get in the way of what was really important.

Less Stress, Better Grades

I have one student who is very conscientious and often very intense—sometimes to the point of making herself physically ill worrying about her projects and her grades. Toward the end of this past quarter, she missed a few days of school, and she seemed to be under some kind of stress to the extent that she was not turning in her homework or making up the work she had missed. She came to me and said, "I just don't know what to do. The quarter is ending. I have a lot of work I haven't gotten done. I don't know what I'm going to do for grades." And she wasn't just talking about my class; she was talking about all of her classes.

So I said, "What's your Goal? Do you want to finish the work? Do you want to get good grades? Or do you want to take an 'Incomplete' for your classes? What is it you're trying to accomplish?" So we spent a few minutes talking about it, and she decided that she really did want to finish the work.

Then we moved to Reality. She just kept saying, "I'm missing all this work! I'm missing all this work!" And I said, "Exactly what is the work that you're missing? Tell me what it is for each class." And it turned out that when she tried to articulate it, she wasn't sure. So as she considered her Options, it became clear to her that the best Way Forward was to take a step back and say,

"Okay, if what I want is to finish the work, then I have to first find out what work I'm missing and then move forward with seeing if I can complete it and raise my grades."

So she walked out of the conversation with a couple of tasks that were enough for her to feel comfortable that she had things under control again. The whole conversation only took about ten minutes. When she came to class the next day, I asked her how things had gone. She said she'd had a very positive conversation with each of her teachers, and she had discovered that she was actually missing far less than she had thought. So the "Reality" she had been dealing with and that had caused her so much frustration hadn't even been real!

Which Guy Should I Date?

I was at the airport with a young woman who was a peer of mine. We'd just been to a training program, and during the whole trip she'd been talking about these two guys she was dating and how frustrated she was because she couldn't decide between them. And this had been going on for six months.

Finally, I could tell she wasn't going anywhere with this, and I had just about had enough. So as we sat there at the airport restaurant, I just jumped in with the GROW questions. "Well, what's happening?" "What have you tried so far?" "What's working and what hasn't worked?" "What's going to happen if you don't do anything about this?"

Within twenty-five minutes, she came to a clear conclusion about whom she was going to continue to date. She said, "I just can't believe it! I've been wrestling with this for six months, and it's so clear to me now." She'd had some criteria in her brain, but she'd never really sat down and worked through the issues. The very next day she confidently went out and broke up with one of the guys so she could focus on her relationship with the other.

Keeping a Customer; Avoiding a Lawsuit

A longtime customer who had made significant investments in our technology requested a meeting with our company executive team. In order to prepare our upper executives for this meeting, Lee, the territory manager, had gone on-site and talked with this company's leadership to make sure all of the out-standing issues were identified. Then he put together a document outlining what had transpired over the last couple of years in this account. (This is a common practice to make sure everyone is on the same page going into the meeting.) However, when Lee sent this document over to the customer for review, for some reason, Dan, the CTO, became very angry. Lee and I were asked to get on a call with him and figure out where the problem was.

Right from the beginning, Dan was clearly agitated and defensive. Because I'd known him for five years, I knew this was totally out of character. I was so thrown off the loop I was almost speechless. I thought, "Oh my gosh! Where do I go from here?" His company was refusing to acknowledge the document Lee had sent, and it became evident that they were looking to get their attorneys involved. And I could not for the life of me understand why. So I decided to just start through the GROW process.

We began by talking about the Goal. Those of us on both sides wanted to make sure that nobody was caught off guard in the C-level meeting, and in order to do that we needed to make sure that our company understood his company's issues and that his C-levels had a fairly good idea of what our company's position might be. So we agreed that our goal in the conversation would be to figure out how to make that happen.

When we moved to Reality, one of the questions I posed to him was, "What process does your company go through when you're trying to bring your executives up to speed on a customer issue before they go into a meeting?" He said, "We make sure they have all the background information. We make sure all the information is accurate. We try to provide insight concerning what our customer wants to talk about so that our executives don't get caught off guard." He then went right through the list of what Lee had assembled and put into place. I just let him talk. I never jumped in and said, "Well, that's exactly what we've done." I just let him define it.

When we got to Options, I said, "Dan, in a perfect scenario, how would you prepare for a meeting like this? What process would you go through?" Dan outlined what he would do. As he talked, I could feel his tone gradually beginning to change, the tension starting to come out of his voice. At the very end he finally said, "Wow, that's actually what you've done, isn't it?"

We moved into Way Forward and got to the question, "What might get in the way?" (This was almost an hour into what was supposed to have been a thirty-minute call.) It wasn't until this point that it finally came out that the format Lee had used in putting together his document was the same format that this company uses in going into a lawsuit (which was something we had no way of knowing). So when they saw the format of the notes, it immediately put them in a defensive mode. They thought we were considering suing them. But they never said anything about this to us.

So bottom line, it was all about the format. I know this seems like a really small thing for a customer to get hung up on, but it's a great example of how so many times it's those small things that really throw off communication.

By the end of the call, Dan was happy. He said, "You know what? The process you put in place is right on target. This is the way we should go. I need to do a better job communicating internally to our team that they shouldn't misread the format of the document or misunderstand the purpose of it." And he literally came to that conclusion on his own.

So on our end, we never had to change anything. We never had to reformat or resubmit. And all we did during the whole conversation was ask the questions and listen.

An interesting addendum to this story is that right after we hung up, I called Lee (who had just gone through GROW training two days before) to debrief. I said, "Well, that was an interesting call! It didn't start where I thought it was going to start, but we ended up on the right page."

Lee said, "You know, at first, I couldn't figure out what the heck you were doing. And then, about ten minutes into it, I realized that you were using that GROW model. It's amazing! In sixty minutes, you turned this guy from being angry and ready to get attorneys involved to, 'Wow, this is going to be a phenomenal meeting, you guys are right on target and I love this document!' This stuff really works!"

From Helpless to Hopeful Friend

Having recently been exposed to the GROW process, I decided to try using it in a conversation with a friend. This friend—Anna—has had difficult circumstances in her life that have caused her tremendous pain and have led to serious complications, including depression. Many of our conversations in the past had been centered around this depression and her feeling of hopelessness about her situation.

As this particular conversation progressed, I began to feel overwhelmed by the negative cycle she was locked in. Suddenly I realized that maybe using the GROW process could be helpful to both of us. So I changed my approach. I said, "Anna, what is it that you want? What is your Goal?"

She replied, "I want to be happy."

I said, "What have you tried so far to accomplish this goal?"

She explained some of the things she had tried. Because of our background I knew a lot of this already, so we didn't have to go into a big discussion on her past. We had already been there.

"So, in a perfect world where there are no boundaries and you could do anything—anything—what would your life be like?"

"I would be happy. I would be married and have a family. I would not have to work unless I wanted to. And I would feel loved."

"So how can you make that happen? How can you feel that way now?"

"I don't know."

"Remember, this is a perfect world and you can do anything. There are no limits. How can you feel happy?"

"I don't know."

"Your goal is to be happy and feel loved, right?"

"Right."

"And you are in a perfect world and can do anything, right?"

"Right."

"So how can you make yourself feel happy in this world? I know you can do this."

After a pause, Anna said, "Well, since I didn't learn what love really is when I was a child, I think I would read books on how to teach children to love. Then I could teach myself—that child part of me that never grew up with love—how to feel love. I think that's where I could start."

"Does that feel like something you could do now?"

"Yes."

"Do you feel you can act on that decision?"

"Yes."

"Is there anything I can do to help?"

"I don't know."

"Well, I know a few books that may be helpful. Would you like me to e-mail the titles to you?"

"Yes."

"And would you like me to check on your progress in a few weeks?"

"Sure."

Before I knew it, our conversation was over, and it hadn't just been a "dump session." Instead, she had discovered a Way Forward and found some hope.

I feel the conversation helped lift Anna out of her cycle of negative reality and helped motivate her. She felt that she had options. She didn't have to wait for someone to tell her what to do anymore. She could do it on her own.

The Boy on the Stairs

One afternoon after school, I heard some voices in the hallway. It sounded like someone was in trouble, so I left my classroom and found two people sitting on the steps—a boy and a girl—having a serious conversation. It was obviously not a good conversation because both of them were extremely upset. I told them that if they needed a place to come and talk, they were welcome to come in my classroom because I was leaving to go make some copies. They said no, so I made sure they were okay and left.

When I returned, I saw that the boy was by himself, and he was obviously in distress—almost in tears. So I sat down next to him and asked him what was wrong. It was as if someone had turned on the faucet. He was almost sobbing. He had soccer pressures. His father wanted him to play a different sport, and he didn't know if he could keep up with it or be any good at it. His classes were all coming together at the same time with the term papers and tests due, and he didn't know how to handle it. He knew he had to get a job and he didn't know how he was going to fit that in. And to top it all off, his girlfriend just broke up with him. The poor guy was absolutely overwhelmed.

So I found myself just asking him, "What is your objective? What is it that you want?" And we walked through a little bit of a goal-setting process. And then I said, "Well, what's keeping you from doing that? What are the challenges you're facing?" And he shared with me the details of his Reality. I said, "Okay, what are some of the ideas that you have? What could you do about [this]? What could you do about [that]?" He shared some of his ideas.

We ended up walking through the entire GROW model, and after about twenty minutes or so, he had come up with a Way Forward he felt good about. He was going to talk with his father to better understand what his dad felt was important. Then he was going to determine for himself what he felt was important and make the conscious decision to let other things go. He realized there was no way he could do it all.

When I saw this boy a couple of weeks later, he was obviously a lot happier, a lot more peaceful. When I asked how everything was going, he told me that he had acted on the decisions he had made during our conversation and everything was working out.

Frankly, I was amazed. This young man had been a total stranger to me. I had never even seen him before talking with him that day on the steps. But I think the GROW model is so powerful and so elegant in its simplicity that when it's used with sincerity, it always, always brings successful results.

Postscript

The stories I've shared in this chapter are only a few of thousands of similar stories. I continue to be amazed at what people tell me about when, where, and how they've applied this approach.

As evidenced in this last story, some of these people say it much better than I do: This approach is "so powerful and so elegant in its simplicity that when it's used with sincerity, it always, always brings successful results." To me, this is the beauty of inside-out. This simple approach can make a huge performance difference in any arena of life.

Reflective Question

- In what situations in your own life could you apply the principles, paradigm, and process in this book?

Chapter 8: For an exercise that will help you

EXPLORE WAYS TO USE GROW IN MANY AREAS

Access the online community at
Alan-Fine.com

CHAPTER NINE

What Do You Do When . . . ?

Learn all you can from the mistakes of others. You won't have time to make them all yourself.

ALFRED SHEINWOLD,
American bridge champion and author

Although the inside-out approach is simple and most people are able to implement it immediately, there are times when you have to deal with a particularly difficult issue or you just get stuck.

If you and I were sitting together, we could use the inside-out process to help you identify your Goals, Reality, and Options and come up with the best Way Forward for you in dealing with your personal issues. But since we're not, I'd at least like to share with you some insights that have proved helpful to others in addressing the challenges of improving performance through GROW.

Below are some of the most common types of questions I've been asked over the years.

Creating Accountability

"The person I'm trying to help says, 'I can't come up with any Goals' or 'I can't come up with any Options. You're the coach; you tell me what to do.'"

"Tell me what to do!" is a phrase I used to hear often in coaching kids in tennis. They'd play really well in practice, but when the pressure was on, they'd want to abdicate their responsibility for deciding what to do next. They'd want a higher authority to tell them what to do.

Almost everyone has had some kind of similar experience—perhaps in parenting, teaching, or managing employees. The problem is that once you tell someone what to do, accountability starts to go out the window. If it doesn't work—even if it's because the person didn't execute properly—it's your fault. You're the one who told him/her what to do. More subtly, if it *does* work, the performer may do well in the particular instance, but he/she hasn't gained the learning or empowerment to make independent, high-performance choices in the future.

One of the main purposes of the inside-out approach is to help people accept responsibility for their own performance. That's when they really get engaged. That's when they stop blaming and accusing and begin to tap into their own Faith, Fire, and Focus. So a helpful conversation might go something like this:

"You want me to tell you what would be best to help you become a high performer?"

"That's right."

"Okay. I believe that one of the most important things you can do to become a high performer is to learn how to decide for yourself what your goals are. You need to get beyond me having to tell you what your goals should be. So now you have a dilemma. Are you going to do what I told you to do or not?"

No matter how hard it may be (and this is one of the main challenges for a coach), you're almost always better off if you avoid the temptation to simply tell people what to do. It may seem quicker and easier in the moment, and it may temporarily feed your ego. But it won't empower the individual to create consistently high performance.

"Someone I'm trying to help can't see beyond the self-criticism—'I'm not qualified. I don't have the skills. I just can't do this.'"

The first of the only two times I went rock climbing, there was a man about fifty feet up on the rock face, completely frozen. He was holding onto the rock for dear life and, despite the instructor's calm and repeated instructions, he just couldn't seem to move. As the afternoon wore on, the man finally became convinced that he either had to get past his panic or he was going to be on the mountain face all night. It was at that point that he finally began to take action that would get him safely to the ground.

The key to working with someone who is paralyzed by some belief (whether that person is being overpowered by a gorilla or is stuck in an unproductive story) is to help him/her get in touch with reality and the consequences of different choices. You might say, "So what's going to happen if you don't take action? What is the consequence? Is that okay with you?" If he/she says, "No, that's not okay," then you can say, "Well then, let's look at our Options."

For example, suppose an employee has been told that the company is downsizing and she can either take a different position with more responsibility or she will be let go. She doesn't want to be let go, but the thought of the new position terrifies her. She's immobilized. She doesn't know what to do. Figuratively, she's standing there, clinging to the rock face, afraid to move.

You could help her look at her Reality and her Options. "So this new position terrifies you. What is it about the position that terrifies you? Suppose you don't take the position. What will happen? Is that okay with you? Is the terror of the new position better or worse than the terror of being terminated?"

When people realize they have choices and they understand the consequences of those choices, it's easier for them to move beyond the immobilization—to make decisions and move ahead.

"The person I'm trying to help sees her situation as completely hopeless."

Helping someone who initially feels hopeless is a bit like pushing a stalled car to get it moving from a stationary position. It's that initial movement that's the hardest. But once there's a bit of momentum in any direction, the pushing doesn't take as much effort. And when there's enough speed, you can change the direction easily.

The first objective is to shift the belief from "it can't be done" to "maybe there's a possibility here." In other words, help shift the Faith in order to engage the Fire and Focus. One approach is to use empathic listening. You may even need to start in the Reality phase of the process and ask the person to describe what he/she sees as hopeless. Then you could do a bit of probing— "How do you know this is hopeless? What is it that's telling you it's hopeless?"

What you're trying to get at is the mechanism that's causing this person to say, "Here's the event, here's how I'm interpreting it, and this is how it's filtering the following event."

At some point in the conversation, the person will probably get enough off his/her chest that you can say, "Now given what you've said, are you open to the possibility that there may be another way to look at this? If so, what might your goal be?" If you time that question right, it will begin to engage the person's Faith, Fire, and Focus so that he/she can begin to move forward.

"In coaching myself, I find it difficult to hold myself accountable. Nobody else really knows what I do, and it's easy to let myself slide."

Several years ago, I worked with David Feherty who, at the time, was relatively new to the professional golf tour. He was having difficulty committing himself to releasing the club head freely through the ball. He was fine on the practice rounds, but when he played in a tournament he would quit a fraction of a second before impact. As a result, he would push the ball off to the right. Whenever we were together he would say that he really meant to commit to the shot, but he didn't seem to be able to stay with it when the pressure was on.

At one point, I asked him, "If I threatened to blow your brains out if you quit on a shot, would you stay committed?"

Somewhat puzzled, he replied that he would.

I said, "If I promised you £50,000 (almost U.S.$100,000) if you committed fully on each shot irrespective of where the ball went, would you do it?"

"Well, sure," he replied grinning. "I'd make more money doing that than winning this week—and I wouldn't even have to make the cut!"

"So committing is within your control if you absolutely had to do it?"

"Well, yes," he said warily, "I suppose it is."

"Okay," I said, "here's the deal. You write out a check to your favorite charity for £1,000 (or U.S.$2,000) and leave it with me. If you commit on every shot next week, I'll return it to you. But if—for whatever reason—you quit on even one shot, I'll send the check off. Your money will not be in any danger because you've said this is within your conscious control if the stakes are high enough. It will only be in danger if you don't mean to do what it takes to commit." Then I added, "I'm confident that this will help you, but I only want you to agree to it if you're sure you can do it. Once you sign the check, the deal is on and only negotiable with my agreement."

He duly wrote out the check for £1,000 to the Royal Society for the Prevention of Cruelty to Animals. (He also called me a few unrepeatable names as he walked away.)

When I talked with David again one week later, I was talking to the new Italian Open champion. He finally understood what commitment meant—and in his enthusiasm, he told me to go ahead and send the check off anyway.

The point is that we all need a little help now and then to hold ourselves accountable, and involving someone else (perhaps a coach, peer, family member, or friend) is one way to do it. Another way is to clarify what you really want. In the end, you almost always get what you want, so if you're not following through on a commitment, you probably wanted something else more than you wanted to follow through.

I've had this kind of conversation with a number of people I've coached. I've said, "Look, it's okay with me that you didn't follow through. I'm not upset about it. But as your coach, I invite you to look at what's happening here. What you're doing says to me that you want something else more than you want to follow through on what you decided to do."

Some understand right away. Others say, "No, no! I really want to follow through."

"Well," I reply, "your behavior says different."

What gets people through failure to follow-through is getting very clear about what they really want and how much they want it—whether or not they're willing to pay the price.

Managing Your Own Interference

"I worry that my coaching skills are so poor that they will come across as artificial or manipulative to the person I'm trying to help."

Those eight-hundred-pound gorillas in your head will always have something to say about anything you do. The trick in getting past their chatter is to focus on simply following the GROW process—even if you think it's going to be clunky. All the evidence I see is that even when the coach feels awkward in doing it, the performer doesn't experience it that way at all. This is because the GROW questions are not new to the performer. They're questions we all ask already; now we're simply asking them in a disciplined, ordered way that creates more Focus and reduces interference. In fact, you can just read them— even mechanically—and it doesn't come over as manipulative or artificial. Just be up front and make sure your motive is to help.

"Sometimes it's hard for me to see people's potential, and that throws me back to the outside-in approach—'Just listen to me and do what I say!'"

Sometimes it *is* hard to suspend judgment and genuinely see someone's potential. I've got a judge in me that makes decisions about people just like anybody else. It's that eight-hundred-pound gorilla in my head constantly chattering away. But I've learned to not believe everything that gorilla says to me. I make a conscious effort to look beyond what he's saying. I combine the results of that effort with what I know about kids and learning, and that's when I begin to see what's possible.

Everybody has the potential to perform better because *everybody* has a phenomenal ability to learn. We were all born with it—even that person in the organization you may have transferred out because you thought he was a disaster. Once upon a time, that person was a cute little one-year-old, hungry to learn and get into everything. What you're seeing now is a buildup of years of emotional defense against the world.

And as long as you judge him based on that buildup—"Oh, that's Chuck. That's just the way he is"—you're going to be scanning for evidence to validate that belief. It's like what happens when you buy a red car or name your new baby "Aidan." Suddenly, you become amazingly aware of all the red cars on the freeway and all the boys who've recently been named "Aidan." So you'll be scanning for evidence to validate your perception of what you see as the present (not the potential) Chuck. As a result, you will never be able to help him get rid of the interference that's blocking his Faith, Fire, and Focus and contribute most meaningfully to the organization.

What's helpful is to rewrite the story you're telling yourself about Chuck. Look for the learner inside and then look for evidence to validate that. Once you change your belief (or Faith) about Chuck, it will change your feelings about working with him (Fire) and your Focus in helping him.

"I've just been made a manager, but I'm so worried about actually engaging someone in a coaching conversation that I find myself repeatedly avoiding doing so."

You'll want to be very clear about it—do you want to be a manager or not? It's a bit like playing golf. If you're going to be a competitive golfer, you have to be willing to play in the sun or in the rain. You can't play only in the sun. If you're going to be a manager, you need to coach. If you don't want to do that, you might want to think about doing something other than managing.

If you do decide to manage, I suggest you GROW yourself and come up with a Way Forward that will help you engage in coaching conversations. In the process, explore Reality. Come to grips with the fact that managing involves coaching. Consider why it is that you feel uncomfortable about coaching. Maybe you've had some negative experiences in the past, or perhaps you're just nervous about doing something you've never done before.

When you brainstorm Options, you may want to consider the value of practicing a few times with someone outside your working environment before trying it with the people you're responsible for at work. Or think about having an initial noncoaching meeting with each team member to simply get to know him/her better and then begin with the person you feel will be easiest to coach.

When you actually engage in the coaching conversation, try just going through the GROW questions listed on pages 60–61. It's amazing how successful most coaches are when they simply ask those questions. It's also amazing how quickly people gain confidence in their ability to coach. That's one of the benefits of the inside-out approach—it's really straightforward and simple.

"I'm trying to coach someone, but my emotions about a particular issue are so charged, I'm afraid the conversation will turn into an argument."

If you have someone you feel comfortable working with, you might want to get that person to coach you through your emotion. If not, you can go through it yourself. You can answer the questions under "Preparing for an Engagement Conversation" on pages 111–115 or fill out "A Checklist to Prepare for Engagement Conversations" in Appendix B on pages 215–216. You can explore the Reality of your emotion. You can think about what it is, when you feel it, why you feel it, and how you feel it. You can go through your Options—ways you could handle it, things you can do if you feel yourself getting drawn into a black hole. Then you can decide on a Way Forward that will work for you.

As we noted in chapter 6, it's usually helpful to role-play a difficult conversation with someone else before you engage the person with whom you have the issue. If you practice confronting the situation and dealing with the emotion, when it actually happens it's not new. It doesn't surprise you. You have more confidence that you can handle it because you've been through it before.

By focusing on the emotion and dealing with it in advance, you keep it from becoming a distraction.

Following the Process

"I'm going through the GROW process, but the performer keeps making comments about Reality, Options, or Way Forward when we're still supposed to be talking about the Goal."

Often, coaching is like opening a soda bottle that's been shaken up. All the gas comes out first. As human beings, we have a lot of "gas," or interference, and sometimes until it's released, we don't see the problem clearly.

One thing you can do is simply acknowledge what they say, take notes in the relevant quadrant (Goal, Reality, Option, or Way Forward), and then gently guide the performer's focus back to the appropriate section of the GROW model without interrupting his/her flow.

Another thing you can do is to be aware of changes in body language. I frequently have an experience in coaching where a performer will suddenly lean back in his seat, put his hands behind his head, and say, "Wow! Now that I think about it, that's what the problem is!" The implication is that he hasn't thought about it. So when you see the posture change, that's a sign that there's a lot changing inside the person and now is the time to be quiet, to let them sort out whatever is going on inside them. At the appropriate time, you can then shift back to the process and help the performer see Goal, Reality, Options, and Way Forward in light of his new insights.

"No matter how hard I try to move the process along, the person I'm trying to help keeps going back to Reality, trying to explain and/or justify the difficulty of the situation."

Often, the reason people stay in Reality is that they don't feel understood. If this is the case, you might say, "Well, let me play back to you what I think I understand and you can confirm it or not." Often doing that is enough to help someone move on. If not—if the person says, "Yes, I believe you understand," but still keeps coming back to Reality, you might reply, "Well, I'm not sure I'll ever understand. I've played it back to you three times now, and each time you've said, 'Yes, you understand,' but then you continue to repeat the same information to me again. Help me understand what's happening."

Another thing you can do when a person seems stuck in Reality is to ask the person to stand outside of the conversation with you and observe what's happening. "Look, we allocated thirty minutes for this conversation. For the past twenty of them, you've been repeating the same things over and over. If we continue to do that, we're not going to finish this conversation. Is that okay with you?" Based on the response, you could either agree to move on or agree to share the Reality now and meet at another time to discuss Options and a Way Forward.

"The person I'm trying to help keeps making comments that I can clearly tell are not accurate."

Verbal communications often contain what are classified in Neuro-Linguistic Programming as *deletions, distortions,* or *generalizations.* Put simply:

- *Deletions* are about missing information—for example, "It's no better." (*What's no better? No better than what? No better than when?*)
- *Distortions* deal with assumptions and structural inaccuracies. "He has an MBA; he would make a good manager" (*an assumption that may or may not be true*).
- *Generalizations* are sweeping statements that come across as being true in every instance, but in reality are not. "He's never on time." (*Really? He has never, ever, in his entire life been on time?*)

It's important for a coach to recognize deletions, distortions, and generalizations and help the performer work through them. For example, think back to the tennis coaching conversation on pages 42–44. When I asked Jim what he wanted to get out of the session, he said, "I'd like to be able to hit a backhand." That's a generalization. We needed to narrow that down and make the goal specific.

Alan: Now what do you mean by hit a backhand?
Jim: In the court.
Alan: Like anywhere on the other side of the net. Is that what you mean?
Jim: No, I'd really like to hit it on this side of the court in the lines.
Alan: Okay, so that side of the court, over the net, within those lines on the green. And how often would you have to do that?
Jim: Half the time.
Alan: Like five times out of ten?
Jim: Right.

If you don't create that kind of clarity, you'll end up with a "Yes, but . . ." conversation. This used to happen to me all the time. I'd work for half an hour with someone, thinking I'd done a great job, but when I'd ask, "So how are we doing," the person would say, "Well, I'm hitting it in the court more often—but it doesn't have much spin, does it?" So I'd work for another half hour, and the person would say, "Well, yeah, I've got more spin on the ball—but it's not moving fast enough." That's what happens when you have a generalization for a Goal in the beginning. It's hard for the coach; it's hard for the performer. So you work through the generalization and get specificity up front.

It's also important to address deletions, distortions, and generalizations throughout the conversation. Otherwise, you and your performer may both be going down a path of making assumptions, drawing meanings, and acting on conclusions and beliefs that may or may not be accurate.

"When I reach the Options stage and I ask if any of the chosen options interest the person enough to explore further, the person says, "No, not really. I've been whammed so many times, I just don't have the energy and enthusiasm to try again."

You might say, "As I see it, here are our choices. We can choose an option on this list, brainstorm some more, find an expert who might have some other ideas, or leave it alone. Am I missing anything?"

That last question is the one that keeps the accountability with the performer. Faced with these choices, a performer will often get irritated. "Well, I can't leave it alone." And so you play it back for him/her again. "Well, these are the options I see. Help me understand what I'm missing." At that point, the responsibility is clearly with the performer, and he/she will (albeit sometimes begrudgingly) go to one of the options or will say, "Okay, let's try and brainstorm some more."

"The person I'm coaching keeps trying to cram too many Options in the Way Forward. He always comes up with five or six things to do instead of one or two."

You might say, "This looks like an awful lot to bite off. Do you want to consider choosing one or two to start with?" If the answer is, "No, I really want to include all these options," then you might encourage the person to prioritize: "Okay, then let's list them in priority and make sure we're investing the most time and energy on the things that matter most."

On the other hand, if the issue is not critical and you're not seriously concerned, you might just let the person run with it—do the things he/she can and pick up the others later. It's a learning experience. And while it might be somewhat detrimental to a person's Faith, Fire, and Focus to fail to execute an overstuffed Way Forward, it could also be detrimental—maybe even more so—for a coach to insist that the person is likely to fail before he/she even tries. Again, it's a process of learning how to "hit the ball" consistently, and a performer can't do that without discovering what happens if he/she hits it too long or too short.

"When I reach the Way Forward stage, the person gives a reluctant yes, but I know he/she is not really going to follow through."

You could reflect that back to the performer. "In listening to you, my sense is that you don't have a passion and commitment about this Way Forward. Is that accurate?" If the person says yes, you could say, "Okay, what's going on?" Typically, a lack of Fire tells you that that the challenge hasn't been chunked down to the level where the performer thinks he/she can do it and is excited about it. That means you've got more work to do as a coach.

"As the coach, I feel I can clearly see the most effective Way Forward, but the person I'm coaching doesn't come up with it—and when I suggest it as an Option, he doesn't understand it and immediately dismisses the idea."

The reality is that a performer's poor idea will often work better than the coach's great idea simply because there's Faith, Fire, and Focus invested in it.

One manager of a division of a large international firm told me, "I keep learning again and again that what will work is what the individual is committed to make work—even if it may not be the optimum solution. If someone has made the commitment to a solution, then it's going to work . . . or they'll come back and ask for help. If they pursue a solution that I choose and tell them to follow, there's no ownership to sustain it over time."

As coaches, we need to always try to work toward *commitment*, and commitment comes from Faith, Fire, and Focus. A performer will put far more time and energy into commitment to a personally chosen Way Forward than into compliance with one that is imposed. If you can't get commitment, you can always go for compliance, but you'll want to be careful because *compliance* can turn into *defiance* if it's overused.

Also, it's helpful to keep in mind that effectively coaching people is a process—not an event. The goal is not for the person to make a perfect decision in one situation, but for him/her to learn from experience and gain the confidence to make and execute good decisions consistently.

> People are generally better persuaded by the reasons which they have themselves discovered than by those which have come into the mind of others.
>
> BLAISE PASCAL,
> 17th-century French mathematician, physicist, and religious philosopher

"Somebody comes back to me and says, 'I followed through on the Way Forward, but it didn't work.'"

You might start by saying, "Tell me about it. What did you do?" You'd want to find out whether this person implemented the Way Forward in the manner in which you thought he/she was going to or not. And you would want to be very specific.

For example, suppose the person said, "I was going to work on my speech making, and I did that thing about standing tall and focusing on the one or two smilers in the group, and it didn't work." You could ask, "How did you know you stood tall? How do you know you focused on the one or two smilers? What did you do to focus on them?" You would need that data to determine whether or not there was a gap between what this person thought he/she did and what he/she actually did. If there is a gap, you could work on reclarifying the Way Forward and trying again. If there isn't a gap, then you would need to go back and revisit Options.

Keep in mind that if you've done your job well, the person you're trying to help was the one who decided on the Way Forward. It was his/her choice, not yours. Sometimes, learning what choices *don't* work—and why—is the fastest way for a person to get to the ones that *will* work and to learn how to make good decisions in the long run.

Working with Teams

"In working with a team, I explain the GROW process and ask if team members would be willing to use it to solve the issue, and someone says no."

People are typically very agreeable to use the process, particularly because they feel it's simple and transparent and there's no threat. But if someone were to say no, you might ask, "What are your objections?" Maybe this person doesn't understand the process. Or maybe he/she has a tendency to resist anything different or new.

If a brief exploration doesn't reveal a quickly solvable reason, I suggest you not dwell on it publicly because it might result in embarrassment or resentment. Just meet privately with the person to go over his/her concerns.

In the team meeting, probably the best thing to do is to just ask as many of the GROW questions as you can without labeling the process. You may miss out on some of the benefits available when everyone is aware and unified, but the conversation would take place randomly in the four GROW quadrants anyway, and asking the questions will help give some positive direction to the interaction.

"In brainstorming Options with a team, some team members get caught up in really crazy ideas and get invested in them to the degree that it starts to create conflict in the group and egos are on the line."

I was in a situation like this several years ago with the executive team of a multinational company that had brought me in to help for a day. As they interacted with each other, I couldn't believe what I was seeing. They were hemorrhaging millions of dollars a month, and they just kept playing out turf issues. I remember sitting there thinking, "I cannot believe that these people think this is okay, given how much money is at stake."

In a situation like this, you can reflect the team dynamic back to the group. You might say something like, "This is what I see happening. It sounds like some of you are invested in 'This is the Way Forward' and others are invested in 'That is the Way Forward.' I'm using the word *invested* because I can see the amount of emotion that's attached to these Options. But I think what's happening is that we may be losing the group. We may be losing perspective. And it seems to be creating interference. So what would you like to do?" This creates awareness of the problem and puts the group in a position to take responsibility to solve it by making different decisions.

"In trying to coach people through a team meeting, I find they have difficulty agreeing on a Way Forward."

If team members have difficulty agreeing on a Way Forward, keep the accountability on their shoulders. "Okay, we have three different versions of how to solve this. If we spend our time arguing about these different approaches, we're never going to reach the point of moving forward. So what do you want to do?"

Then people have to make a choice—"Do I want to take all this time trying to convince everyone that I'm 'right,' or do I want to do what's going to move this group forward?" Typically, people recognize that although a particular solution might not be their first choice, it is the choice that will unify and move the team ahead, and so they engage in making the choice and in making it successful.

A Final Word

I hope the answers in this chapter will give you ideas as to how you might be able to implement GROW in your own situation. If you ever feel stuck, just go back to the basic principle (Focus) and paradigm (inside-out). Keep in mind that removing interference can have a huge impact on improving performance.

Chapter 9: For an exercise that will help you

LEARN AND SHARE WITH OTHERS

Access the online community at **Alan-Fine.com**

The Faith Behind the Focus and the Fire

Make the most of yourself by fanning the tiny, inner sparks of possibility into flames of achievement.

GOLDA MEIR,
fourth prime minister of the state of Israel

I first met "Divot" at the National Sports Center for Wales in the winter of 1986, where he was training with the other members of the Welsh Amateur Golf Team. Born and raised in a mining town in South Wales, Divot was twenty years old with prematurely gray hair. He came across as introverted and shy, yet he was a paradox. Despite that his nickname implied a distinct lack of intelligence*, he was always asking questions.

I later learned that he had quit school at fifteen—the earliest possible age for doing so in Wales—and had then tried a variety of dead-end jobs, including delivering promotional leaflets door-to-door. Nevertheless, he had a talent for golf that had enabled him to become a member of the national team. Even so, the national coach, who'd asked me to spend the weekend with the team, had taken me aside and said, "Don't waste too much time on this one. He's technically so poor he'll never make it. Besides, he's not the sharpest pencil in the box!"

So there was Divot—obviously uncertain about his place on the team and taking ribbing from the team members and coaches who saw him as being a bit dense. Though I was in no position to assess his technical abilities, by the end of the first day, there was one thing I knew for certain: if ever I saw a learner, this was one. Maybe he learned differently than his classmates had at school.

---

* For nongolfers, a "divot" is the small lump of grass and dirt players tear out of the ground when hitting the ball.

Maybe he learned differently than his teammates did on the golf course. But despite his discomfort, he was there, asking question after question and displaying all the symptoms of a rabid learner. So not only did I try to respond to his questions throughout the weekend; I continued to do so after the team event.

The more I engaged with Divot, the clearer it became to me that he had plenty of Fire. What we needed to address was his Focus and his Faith. Up to that point, he'd been focused on what he thought others believed about him, and their opinions had formed the basis of what he believed about himself. What we needed to do was help him shift his attention to something that would help him change his belief about himself.

As we worked together over the next few years, our Way Forward included three areas of Focus. First, to keep his mind quiet as he hit the ball, he would focus on saying "back" when his club reached the top of his backswing and "hit" when the clubface hit the ball. Second, to keep his mind quiet when he wasn't hitting the ball, he would focus on maintaining a confident and upright posture—the same posture he had when he played well. And third, to change his belief about himself in general, he would focus on changing some things he was paying attention to that were giving him negative messages— things such as going on the professional tour and having to park his ten-year-old broken-down Ford beside Nick Faldo's new sports car, or wearing clothes that didn't have sponsors' logos on them, or walking into the clubhouse at his local course after missing a tournament cut and hearing people say, "Well, you didn't do very well last week, did you?" We figured out a way to get him a car and clothes that sent a more positive message, and we worked to develop ways to respond when people said things that triggered his insecurities.

What enabled him to develop and carry out these options was creating an environment in which he felt safe to process his own experience without fear of judgment or being pushed. The more we were able to remove the interference to his Faith, Fire, and Focus, the more his learning increased and the more his performance improved.

After Divot's first season on the professional tour, the two of us sat in a small room at a golf club outside London reviewing the year. As he began to talk about his experience over the past few months, he began to choke up. He said, "Do you think I should quit? I've won six thousand quid (about U.S. $10,000). That's beyond my wildest dreams. Surely it's not going to get any better than this!"

But Divot was wrong. It did get better. As he continued to work on shifting his Focus from all the interference—the self-doubts, the negative comments of some of his former teachers, the mocking remarks of other golfers—to what he came to call his "tasks" (his chosen Ways Forward), his Faith continued to improve. He began to gain confidence in his ability to perform consistently and well. His scores improved. His goals and his winnings became bigger. We spent less time talking about how to deal with people. And his Fire grew even more.

At the time of this writing, Divot had placed in the top ten thirty-nine times and taken first place three times on the European Tour, represented his country nine times in the World Cup, and been featured in the top 50 of the Official World Golf Rankings. He was also ranked in the top 40 of the all-time money winners on the PGA European Golf Tour. Most impressively, in the 2002 Ryder Cup Matches*, he beat Phil Mickelson (then ranked number two in the world) to win an invaluable point and a historic victory for Europe—and he did it despite a previous a year of misery created by repeated suggestions from the British press that he should resign from the team.

In case any of you golfaholics haven't already guessed, Divot is professional golfer Phil Price. And to me, Phil is a prime example of discovering and doing what's possible. Who would have thought that a shy, "slow," socially challenged young man who walked with his shoulders slumped and didn't look you in the eye would turn out to be a multimillion-dollar golf winner as well as a loving husband and devoted father of two? I have to admit that even as much as I believe in the learner inside everyone, I never would have guessed it myself.

> **Limitations live only in our minds.**
>
> JAMIE PAOLINETTI,
> American cycling
> champion

Phil is the first to admit that, taken to the extreme, his questioning nature has sometimes actually undermined his Faith, Fire, and Focus. He can ask so many questions that it becomes difficult for him to settle down, be present in the here and now, and keep a quiet mind. As the saying goes, "Any strength taken to excess can become a weakness." But for the most part, the learner inside Phil has led him to a path of discovering and doing what's possible.

To me, this is the fascination of the inside-out approach—the possibility

* The Ryder Cup competition is a biennial golf event between teams from Europe and the United States.

and greatness that lie within every individual. And this is the joy—helping ourselves and others discover and fulfill that potential. It's not in gaining or dispensing new Knowledge. It's not in the "I have it and you don't, so I'm going to give it to you and you need to do what I say" approach. It's not in giving criticism—even positive criticism—or in evaluating or judging. It's not in getting people to press harder on the gas pedal.

> **What wine is so sparkling, what so fragrant, what so intoxicating as possibility!**
>
> SØREN KIERKEGAARD,
> 19th-century
> Danish philosopher
> and theologian

It's in getting people to take their foot off the brake. It's in making it safe for them to learn from their own experience. It's in removing the interference that gets in the way of releasing Knowledge, Faith, Fire, and Focus. These are the things that drive us to be and do our very best.

Your Own Way Forward

From the 10X girl to Stephen Ames and his $1.4 million win to CEO's, managers, leaders, teachers, musicians, parents, and others whose stories I've included in this book, you've seen the breakthrough power of the inside-out approach. You've now reached the point where you determine your own Way Forward. You decide what to do about what you've read.

> **Dwell in possibility.**
>
> EMILY DICKINSON,
> 19th-century
> American poet

I sincerely hope the paradigm (inside-out), the principle (Focus), and the process (GROW) in this book will give you what you need to create breakthrough performance in your own life and to help others create breakthrough performance in theirs. For me, these things constitute critical Knowledge in the area of human-performance improvement.

If you determine to act on this Knowledge, the GROW process itself can help you decide how to best implement it in your unique situation. It can help you clarify your Goal, understand the Realities you're dealing with, identify your Options, and determine a Way Forward that will work for you. It can help you get rid of the interference that's getting in the way of your doing what it takes to be great.

My experience in working with people over the years has convinced me of this: ***The finest service we can give to other human beings is to make it safe for them to explore their own experience.***

This is when people begin to reconnect with their Faith, Fire, and Focus. This is when they begin to dare to dream, to think about what's possible. This is when transformations and breakthroughs happen.

The Faith, Fire, and Focus inside *you* is something that is truly amazing, and your ability to release it in yourself and others will not only transform you and those you help; it will transform the world.

My best to you on the journey!

Chapter 10: For an exercise that will help you
DISCOVER AND DO WHAT'S POSSIBLE
Access the online community at
Alan-Fine.com

APPENDIX A

THE MANAGER'S GROW SHEET

Below are the notes written by Eric, a new manager, as he used GROW to work though a difficult issue in his training company (story on pages 61–63).

GOAL

What issue do I want to work through?

How to provide enough leads for all of the regional sales people in a way that is affordable, doesn't waste leads, and doesn't overload a phenomenal business developer.

What do I want from this GROW session? (What's my S.M.A.R.T. Goal?)

A plan that will allow me to hold four well-attended opens in each of the seven regions per year and to keep the cost of filling these opens within the industry standard.

What are the consequences if I do not take action?

We'll limit our growth because we won't have enough lead generation for each of the regions; or

I'll be paying way more than the industry standard for lead generation; or

The inequity in the number of participants between programs filled by Scott and those filled by others will continue to throw some account managers into overload and cause others to feel their regions are getting the short end of the deal.

REALITY

Briefly, what's been happening?

"Opens" have been the primary source of new leads for the company.

Scott has been doing 90 percent of the work on setting up the opens. If he gets hit by a bus or gets burned out and wants to move on, we'll be in deep trouble.

Through a commission rate that increases with each additional five participants, Scott is incented to get as many people as he can into each program. With the scaled percentage increase per participant, it would theoretically be possible for him to reach the point where he is earning more than we're charging for the program.

Scott does a lot of things manually, which makes his approach hard to replicate with others.

What have I tried so far?

Giving Scott more "opens" to fill.

Hiring others to do the same job.

What were the results?

Scott is getting maxed out. It is unlikely that he could handle any more programs.

Others we've hired to do the same job perform at about 30 percent of Scott's level.

Some "opens" (the ones assigned to Scott) have had too many participants for the sales reps to effectively follow up on; others (assigned to other people) have been canceled because there weren't enough attendees.

We've been paying Scott significantly more than the industry standard for business development, but if we lose Scott, we're going to be in big trouble.

The people we've hired have found it hard to get motivated by Scott's manual approach. When they suggest automating certain procedures, Scott says, "You'll lose the personal touch and that will impact your results."

What's my sense of the obstacles for me? For others (if others are involved)?

"Opens" are expensive.

Scott is definitely a star player, but his compensation plan is not aligned with the needs of the company.

The cost of hiring additional business developers is high, ramp-up is difficult, and performance is poor compared to Scott's.
Scott's goal is to make as much money as possible—even more than he is making now.

I need to be a good manager and keep costs as low as possible, and at the same time do what can be done to drive growth.

In what different ways might others describe this situation?
I really don't know. Maybe I should ask.

Is my Goal still realistic?
It has to be realistic. I have to figure out an answer. I may not know what I need to do now, but we absolutely must expand our sales pipeline affordably.

OPTIONS

Describe fantasyland—If I could do anything to make progress on this issue, what might I do?
Have several lead-generation pipelines in place—not just "opens."

Tell Scott he can only do so many "opens"; if he wants to earn more, move him on to being a client manager.

Take more time to figure out the problem. Get more information to make sure my perception of reality is accurate.

Talk with Scott and get his thoughts and feelings. Find out why he's so good.

Talk to Scott's peers. Find out why they are struggling in the role. (Are they really struggling, or are they just performing at an average level compared to Scott?)

Talk to some of the other client managers who benefit from the "opens" and try to see what they're seeing.

Talk to the sales team.

Challenge my perception that Scott is maxed out.

Challenge my perception that I should pay only a certain level of compensation for somebody in this role. Maybe it would be more efficient to pay Scott an untraditionally high income than it would be to pay for salaries and benefits for others.

Help Scott increase his capacity by delegating some of the manual things he's doing, such as list building and administrative work.

Schedule even more "opens" with Scott, but change the compensation so that instead of putting 60 people in 18 opens, he is incented to put 35 to 40 people into 28 opens, spreading his performance more evenly over all the regions.

If others are involved, what would they see or hear to get their attention?

Although my decision will ultimately impact others, I'm not trying to influence anyone in the decision-making process, so this question really does not apply.

If I were watching myself work through this issue, what would I recommend?

Reach out to some of my colleagues outside the company who are running their own firms, find out what they are doing with people in this role, and see what they would suggest.

Do any of these Options interest me enough to explore further?

Yes—especially those that involve taking more time to figure out the problem and challenging my own perceptions.

If I were to act on this/these chosen Option(s), how might I go about it?

Immediately:

> *Benchmark with colleagues outside the company.*

> *Explore the possibilities of changing Scott's compensation.*

> *Explore ways (automation or administrative help) that might help Scott leverage his efforts.*

In the near future:

> *Continue to develop a more robust marketing strategy. Hire a marketing director to manage additional lead-generation activities, including trade shows, webinars, mailers, and facilitator support.*

WAY FORWARD

Do/does this/these Option(s) interest me enough to take action?
Yes!

How will I go about it?
Take the immediate steps (above) now; GROW future steps after resolving this issue.

What might get in my way?
Nothing significant. I can do these things. They may or may not give me all the answers, but there really are no barriers to moving forward except for my own mental interference; i.e.:

> *"If Scott is not motivated, he might decide to move on."*

> *"Scott will essentially be the only driving force behind filling our 'open' programs. Something might happen to him—he could still get hit by a bus."*

> *"If we end up providing administrative help, the fact that Scott has never managed anyone before could be a challenge. When he runs into obstacles in trying to delegate, he may go into his typical reaction, which is just to do it himself."*

How might I overcome that?
Focus on the immediate next steps—set up the calls and/or meetings and gather ideas. Don't try to manage a solution yet.
Down the road:

> *Set up the compensation so that Scott will be incented to perform in the way we need him to perform—and will also enable him to make even more money.*

> *Be with Scott when he sets up the expectations for his administrative help (if we go that route). Stay with him and show him how to manage for the first few weeks.*

> *Pray that Scott doesn't get hit by that bus!*

What and when is my next step?
Set up appointments to talk with colleagues outside the company this week and validate or change my perceptions.

Set up an appointment with Scott.

APPENDIX B

THE INSIDEOUT
PERFORMANCE TOOL KIT

Questions to Use in Breakthrough Conversations

The questions below are helpful in conducting a breakthrough (or performer-driven) conversation when the person you're trying to help is aware of the issue and willing to engage in a conversation about it. The purpose is to help the performer achieve breakthrough on his/her issue (see pages 87–97).

GOAL

What topic do you want to discuss?
What do you want from this discussion? (What's your S.M.A.R.T. Goal?)
What are the consequences if you do not reach this Goal?

REALITY

Briefly, what's been happening?
What have you tried so far?
What were the results?
What's your sense of the obstacles for you? For others (if others are involved)?
Is the Goal still realistic?

OPTIONS

Describe fantasyland—if you could do anything, what might you do?
If you were the other person/people, what would you have to hear/see to

get your attention (assuming others are involved)?

If you were watching this conversation, what would you recommend?

Would you like suggestions from me?

Do any of these ideas interest you enough to explore further?

If you were to do this, how might you go about it?

WAY FORWARD

Does this Option interest you enough to take action?

How will you go about it?

What might get in the way?

How might you overcome that?

What and when is the next step?

Questions to Use in Engagement Conversations

The questions below are helpful in conducting an engagement (or coach-driven) conversation when the person you're trying to help is unaware of the issue and/or unwilling to engage in a conversation about it. The purpose is to engage the person in a breakthrough conversation (see pages 105–122).

GOAL

Explain your Goal

"I have something I'd really like your help with. Can we discuss it now? If not, when?

"My problem involves my perception of . . . Is it still okay to discuss this now?

Share your intentions

"I'd like to tell you how this appears to me, and I want to understand how it appears to you. If I'm accurate, I want to work with you to change things. If I'm not accurate, I want to understand what is happening."

REALITY

Share your Reality

"This is my perception."

Demonstrate your understanding

"So what you're saying is . . ."

"What you're feeling is . . ."

"Have I understood you correctly?"

OPTIONS

Describe choices

"I am trying to resolve this in the most positive way possible for both of us, and if you choose not to work with me on this, I will have no choice but to . . ."

WAY FORWARD

If the person agrees to engage . . .

Move to a performance discussion to resolve the issue.

If the person refuses to engage . . .

Carry out your predetermined alternative.

A Checklist to Prepare for Engagement Conversations

Because engagement conversations can be difficult, it's important to prepare in advance. Below is a checklist of things you can do to prepare (see pages 111–115).

Clarify your thinking (GROW yourself)

☐ Recognize your own issue.

☐ What will get the performer's attention?

☐ What will you do if you can't get the performer's attention?

Plan the conversation

☐ Keep the S.M.A.R.T. Goal for the conversation in mind.

☐ Identify language for each phase of the conversation.

☐ Anticipate the performer's possible responses.

Conduct the conversation

☐ Share your intentions—repeatedly.

☐ Identify language for each phase of the conversation.

☐ Demonstrate understanding.

☐ Ask for buy-in—repeatedly.

Feedback Questions

Below are three questions you can ask in giving feedback that will help remove interference and keep accountability with the person you're trying to help (see pages 128–132).

What worked?
Where did you get stuck?
What would you do differently next time?

GROW Questions for Groups or Teams

Below are questions that are helpful in working through issues as a team (see pages 144–150).

GOAL

What topic do we want to discuss?

What do we want from this discussion? (What's our S.M.A.R.T. Goal?)

What are the consequences if we do not reach this Goal?

REALITY

Briefly, what's been happening?

What have we tried so far?

What were the results?

What's our sense of the obstacles for us? For others (if others are involved)?

Is the Goal still realistic?

OPTIONS

Describe fantasyland—if we could do anything, what might we do?

If others are involved, what would they need to see or hear to get their attention?

If we were watching this conversation, what would we recommend?

Do any of these ideas interest us enough to explore further?

If we were to do this, how might we go about it?

WAY FORWARD

Does this Option interest us enough to take action?

How will we go about it?

What might get in the way?

How might we overcome that?

What and when is the next step?

ACKNOWLEDGMENTS

In my continuing journey, there have been many people who have been the proverbial "wind beneath my wings." Some have opened doors for me; some have changed my life.

I would like to especially thank the following people:

- Rebecca Merrill, whose patience, research, synergy, and expertise in English (which was hard for me to admit) have finally drawn this book out of me, after many before her failed.
- Peter Lewis, Wally Cole, and John Crooke, without whose help and encouragement I would never have kept playing tennis and found my vocation.
- Tim Gallwey, whose insights into the minds of tennis players turned my thinking about performance upside down and showed me how to apply the theoretical psychology I found so fascinating.
- Graham Alexander and John Whitmore, lifelong friends who both challenged and inspired me, and in partnership with whom the first iteration of the GROW model was created.
- Helga Kahnert, who changed my life by showing me I wasn't OK—and that it really was OK that I wasn't OK.
- Tim Reeder, Margaret McIntyre, Deborah Allen-Baber, Jim Moore, Ben Cannon, and Stephen Bamfylde—all of whom recognized abilities in me that I never saw.
- Buster Mottram, Phil Kenyon, Gary Cullen, Colin Montgomery, David Llewellyn, Phillip Price, Stephen Ames—all athletes from whom I learned a great deal more than they did from me; and especially David Feherty, whose public lunacy and endorsement of our work together amazingly still seems to give me credibility.
- George Knight, for the patience, intelligence, and sense of humor he has shared with me, both as a colleague and, more importantly, as a true friend.

- Kim Capps, whose ongoing encouragement and help with content development and refinement have been invaluable.
- Jacques Bazinet, for his helpful feedback and perspective.
- My colleagues at InsideOut, who helped in the development, testing, and refining of this material and lent their talents to support this book effort in a variety of ways.
- Dr. Bruce Jackson of the Utah Valley University Center for the Advancement of Leadership—particularly for his research in the area of "flow"—and the research interns provided by the Center.
- Tony Daloiso, Shane Cragun, and Kendall Lyman, who provided feedback and additional insight regarding the application of this material in the organizational setting.
- My friends at Root Learning—particularly Victor Zhang—for sharing their unique perspective and creativity.
- Roger Merrill, for his insight and encouragement.
- Mary E. Wentz, for transcribing endless hours of recorded conversation.
- Adrian Zackheim, Adrienne Schultz, Brooke Carey, and all at Penguin Portfolio who helped turn the manuscript into a published work.
- All who shared their personal experiences with me concerning the paradigm, principle, and process in this book. Whether or not their stories were finally included, each had an influence on the final result.

Most of all, I would like to thank Penny and our children, Timothy and Kristen, who have not only tolerated my Fire for the content in this book and my bizarre travel schedule in sharing it with others but have also showed me there really is more in life. Tim and Kristen, you grew up to make us proud, in spite of my experiments with you.

NOTES

Chapter 1: A Blinding Glimpse of the Obvious

1. Jeffrey Pfeffer and Robert I. Sutton, *The Knowing-Doing Gap: How Smart Companies Turn Knowledge into Action* (Boston: Harvard Business Publishing, 2000), 1.
2. Ibid., 25. See also Sidney Finkelstein, *Why Smart Executives Fail;* Larry Bossidy and Ram Charan, *Execution*; and Ken Blanchard, Paul Meyer, and Dick Ruhe, *Know Can Do!*
3. This formula is an adaptation of Tim Gallwey's reference to "Performance equals Potential minus Interference" or "P = P – I."

Chapter 2: The Nature of Performance

1. Curt Coffman and Gabriel Gonzalez-Molina, *Follow This Path: How the World's Greatest Organizations Drive Human Potential* (New York: Warner Books, 2002), 129.
2. Gordon MacKenzie, *Orbiting the Giant Hairball* (New York: Viking, 1998), 19–20.
3. "On Giants' Shoulders; Millennium Edition," Times Educational Supplement, December 31, 1999, http://www.summerhillschool.co.uk/pages/school_policies.html.
4. A. S. Neill, *Summerhill School: A New View of Childhood,* rev. ed. (New York: St. Martin's Griffin, 1995), 9.
5. "Report of an Inquiry Into Summerhill School—Leiston, Suffolk, January 2000 (Part One)," http://paed.com/summerhill/summ/sml.htm.
6. Biographical information on former Summerhill students is from "Report of an Inquiry into Summerhill School; Leiston, Suffolk; January 2000 (Part One)," http:// paed.com/summerhill/summ/sml.htm.

7. Carol Dweck, "The Effort Effect," *Stanford*, March/April 2007, http://www.stanfordalumni.org/news/magazine/2007/marapr/features/dweck.html.

8. John P. Kotter and Dan S. Cohen, *The Heart of Change* (Boston: Harvard Business School Press, 2002), 2.

9. Rick Reilly, "Strongest Dad in the World," *Sports Illustrated*, June 20, 2005.

10. Ibid.

11. "The Execution Quotient: A Measure of What Matters" (white paper, FranklinCovey, 2004), 3.

12. Larry Bossidy and Ram Charan, *Execution: The Discipline of Getting Things Done* (New York: Crown Business, 2002), 69.

Chapter 3: Getting Rid of Interference

1. Kathleen D. Ryan and Daniel K. Oestreich, *Driving Fear Out of the Workplace: Creating the High-Trust, High-Performance Organization* (San Francisco: Jossey-Bass, 1998), 3–4.

2. Rosamund Stone Zander and Benjamin Zander, *The Art of Possibility: Transforming Professional and Personal Life* (Penguin, 2002), 29–30.

3. Mihaly Csikszentmihalyi, *Creativity: Flow and the Psychology of Discovery and Invention* (New York: HarperCollins, 1996), 110.

4. Csikszentmihalyi, *Flow: The Psychology of Optimal Experience* (New York: HarperCollins, New York, 1991), 53–54.

5. Csikszentmihalyi, *Finding Flow* (New York: Basic Books, 1997), 31.

Chapter 4: Creating Focus Through "GROW"

1. Velocity: "The speed and direction of motion of a moving body," *The American Heritage Science Dictionary* (Boston: Houghton Mifflin, 2005).

2. Adapted from ProjectSmart.co.uk.

Chapter 5: Coaching for Breakthrough

1. Marshall Goldsmith, "Helping Successful People Get Even Better," *Business Strategy Review* (Spring 2003).

2. Transcribed from NBC telecast of the Tournament Players Championship, March 26, 2006.

3. Ibid.

4. *Coaching Conundrum 2: The Heart of Coaching*, http://www.blessingwhite .com/content/reports/coachingconundrum2.pdf, 4, 9.

5. Denise Wright, "Global Trends in Coaching," *humanCapital*, April–May 2006, 83.

6. *Coaching Conundrum 2: The Heart of Coaching*, http://www.blessingwhite .com/content/reports/coachingconundrum2.pdf, 8.

7. Marcus Buckingham, *First Break All The Rules* (New York: Simon & Schuster, 1999), 28.

8. Ibid., 31–32.

9. William Oncken and Donald L. Wass, "Who's Got the Monkey?," *Harvard Business Review*, Nov.–Dec. 1974, 75–80.

10. Jeffrey Schwartz and David Rock, "The Neuroscience of Leadership," *strategy+business* webinar, November 2, 2006, http://www.strategy-business .com/webinars/webinar/webinar-neuro_lead.

11. Schwartz and Rock, "The Neuroscience of Leadership," *strategy+business*, Summer 2006, http://www.strategy-business.com/press/article/06207.

12. Schwartz and Rock, "The Neuroscience of Leadership," *strategy+business* webinar, 2006.

13. Schwartz and Rock, "The Neuroscience of Leadership," *strategy+business*, Summer 2006.

14. Barbara Pease and Allan Pease, *The Definitive Book of Body Language* (New York: Bantam, 2004), 9.

Chapter 6: Coaching for Engagement

1. Stephen R. Covey, *The 7 Habits of Highly Effective People* (New York: Simon & Schuster, 1989), 241.

Chapter 7: Inside-out in Teams and Organizations

1. Eric Hausman, "Louis Gerstner, Chairman & CEO, IBM, ChannelWeb, http://www.crn.com/it-channel/18827440.

2. Polly LaBarre, "Marcus Buckingham Thinks Your Boss Has an Attitude Problem," *Fast Company*, July 2001, http://www.fastcompany.com/ magazine/49/buckingham.html.

3. "Only One in Three Employees Engaged" (press release, BlessingWhite,

April 24, 2008), http://www.blessingwhite.com/docDescription.asp?id=229&pid=6&sid=1.

4. "Towers Perrin Study Finds Significant 'Engagement Gap' Among Global Workforce" (press release, Towers Perrin, October 22, 2007), http://www.towersperrin.com/tp/showdctmdoc.jsp?url=HR_Services/United_States/Press_Releases/2007/20071022/2007_10_22.htm&country=global.

INDEX

Paolinetti, Jamie, 204
parents, 6, 28, 48
  and accountability, 79, 187
  as coaches, 69, 71–72, 80
  and engagement conversations, 109,
    112–13, 125
  and Faith, Fire, and Focus, 19–21, 23,
    32–33
  and GROW, 51, 57–58, 164
  and interference, 38, 107
  use inside-out approach, 124–26
  See also families
Pascal, Blaise, 198
passion, 16, 27, 29, 33, 69–70, 74, 135,
    158, 197. *See also* Fire
Patton, Bruce, 112
Pease, Allan, 94
Pease, Barbara, 94
performance
  critical elements of, 30, 52
  definition of, 52
  improvement experts, 14
  management, 58, 71
  under pressure, 12–13, 15
performing arts, 6, 12, 23, 28, 37, 41,
    114, 164
Pfeffer, Jeffrey, 6
planning, 113, 132–33, 135–37, 193
Pliny The Elder, 8
practice, 13, 25, 30, 45, 113–14, 192–93
presentations, 24, 26, 56–57
Price, Phil, 204
priorities, 29, 90, 94, 136, 157–58,
    171–72, 197
psychologists, 4, 14, 20, 25. *See also*
    individual names
public speaking, 56–57

Reality
  and coaching, 83, 89, 131–32, 194
  explanation of, 64–67
  See also GROW

right/wrong mechanism, 110, 120, 134–36
Rock, David, 86
Ryan, Kathleen, 39

salespeople, 17, 29, 38–39, 51, 58–59, 61
SayDoCo, 140–43, 145, 148, 150–51,
    157–59
schools. *See* classroom; education; teachers
Schuller, Robert H., 24
Schwartz, Jeffrey, 86
self
  assessing, 131
  awareness, 105
  esteem, 166
  interference, 4–5
Semler, Ricardo, 78
Sheinwold, Alfred, 186
S.M.A.R.T. (Specific, Meaningful,
    Actionable, Realistic, Time-phased)
    Goals
  and coaching, 79, 83, 88, 96, 137, 207
  explanation of, 63–64
  successful examples of, 164, 166, 169
  and teams/organizations, 145, 147–50
  and the Way Forward, 66–67, 96, 148
sports
  coaching of, 3–5, 8–9, 11–15, 21, 30, 48,
    68–76, 78, 165–68
  and Faith, Fire, and Focus, 157
  and GROW, 57, 165–66
  and interference, 46
  See also athletes
"state of flow." *See* flow, state of
students, 11, 48
  and accountability, 79
  and breakthrough conversations, 113–14
  coaching of, 69, 75
  and Faith, Fire, and Focus, 35
  and fear of grades, 40
  and GROW, 179–80, 184–85
  at Summerhill, 22–23
  and watch-out mode, 20

ABOUT THE AUTHOR

ALAN FINE is the founder and president of InsideOut Development, an innovative and fast-growing professional-services firm offering training, executive-coaching, and organizational-consulting services. In addition to being a popular trainer and speaker, Alan has spent the last twenty-five years as a mental performance/focus coach to top professional golfers, tennis players, musicians, and corporate executives.

Alan is considered by many to be one of the fathers of the modern executive-coaching movement. Twenty-five years ago, he helped develop a basic performance model, known as GROW, which is now a gold-standard approach used by executive coaches and organizational-design experts worldwide. InsideOut Development makes not only this model but also its powerful underlying mind-set and accompanying practical implementation tools available to a broad audience.

In addition to being used with top athletes in a variety of sports, the InsideOut approach to coaching and breakthrough performance has been used for over two decades by some of the most well-respected companies in the world, including Yum Brands, New Balance, GE, IBM, Procter & Gamble, Walgreens, and many others.

Alan first became interested in the science of coaching in the field of sports where he has worked with David Feherty, Colin Montgomerie, Philip Price, Stephen Ames, and many other Ryder Cup and PGA champions. In this capacity, he has been a contributing columnist for *Golf International Magazine* and has published two books, *Inside Out Golf* and *Play to Win Golf* (with David Feherty). In addition to his work consulting with Fortune 500 leaders, Alan is very much in demand as a speaker and thought leader, where he incorporates an engaging mix of humor and commentary drawn from the performance-driven world of the professional athlete.

To learn more about Alan, go to www.alan-fine.com/alan

REBECCA R. MERRILL is coauthor with Dr. Stephen R. Covey and Roger Merrill of the *New York Times* best seller *First Things First* and is coauthor with Roger Merrill of *Life Matters* and *Connections.* She also provided assistance to Dr. Covey on *The 7 Habits of Highly Effective People* and *The 7 Habits of Highly Effective Families* and assisted Dr. Covey's son, Stephen M. R. Covey, with *The Speed of Trust.*

HISTORY OF THE GROW MODEL

Twenty-five years ago, Alan Fine codeveloped the GROW Model with two colleagues, John Whitmore and Graham Alexander, resulting in each having joint interest in the work. The basic GROW model is an acronym for the four stages of decision making and is considered today by many executive coaches worldwide to be a gold-standard framework for structuring coaching conversations.

Over the past 20 years, Alan and his firm, InsideOut Development LLC, have developed and expanded their content, including significant enhancements to and derivatives of the original GROW Model. As a result of this effort, InsideOut Development's version of the original model has been differentiated in the marketplace, one example of its uniqueness being the use of the term "Way Forward" as the fourth step in the GROW Model.

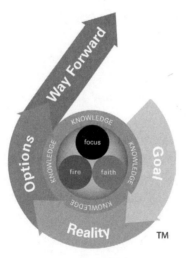

This enhanced GROW Model has been integrated into InsideOut Development's expanding array of training programs, application tools, job aids, and other original content. The enhancements and derivatives are not part of the work developed by the original partners and are solely the property of InsideOut Development.

To learn more about the GROW model, go to
www.alan-fine.com/grow

ABOUT INSIDEOUT DEVELOPMENT

InsideOut Development is a professional services firm that provides leadership, management, and front-line employee training programs; executive coaching services; team performance workshops; and organizational consulting services to a large global clientele. The company, recognized as a leader in developing manager-as-coach skills, trains tens of thousands of people annually using the GROW Model and other innovative tools and programs developed by Alan Fine and the InsideOut Development team.

The company also provides train-the-trainer certification and has certified thousands of facilitators in its programs. InsideOut Development's products and services have been used by hundreds of business and industry leaders, including many of the Fortune 500, such as Westinghouse, Sodexo, Oracle, Kraft, and NASA.

These products and services help organizations achieve the following types of breakthrough performance:

- Uniting executive teams in their strategic direction and aligning systems and structures in their organization.
- Providing managers and team leaders with tools for unlocking team performance.
- Improving any area of individual employee performance, such as customer service, sales effectiveness, project management, product development, R&D, etc.
- Increasing empowerment, engagement, accountability, and trust in the organization.

To learn more about InsideOut Development, go to www.insideoutdev.com/aboutiod